Praise for *The Art of Being Human at Work*

"Work does not have to suck. What is more, work can even be a dojo for joy, learning, and immense personal growth. Let Ali—who is both a horse and human whisperer—show you how." —**Dan Harris, author of *10% Happier* and host of the 10% Happier podcast**

"Compiling over ten years of coaching expertise and a lifetime's worth of wisdom, Allison Schultz's *The Art of Being Human at Work* provides a guide for managers, and all of us really, to bring our heart and our humanity into the workplace, creating the possibility for a more compassionate and awakened sense of being at work." —**Sharon Salzberg, author of *Lovingkindness* and *Real Life***

"As a co-founder of Reboot, Ali Schultz has spent a decade on the front lines of leadership development. This wonderfully well-written book is a collection of reports from the front, all of them exploring "the art of being human at work." The reports are brief but packed with insight, each of them worthy of taking time for deep reflection. If you are looking for leadership literature that goes beyond tips, tricks, and techniques to speak to the heart of the matter, this gem of a book will serve you well." —**Parker J. Palmer, author of *Let Your Life Speak*, *A Hidden Wholeness*, and *On the Brink of Everything***

"This must-read book for all leaders and aspiring leaders will show you how to learn from your difficult emotions and most challenging life experiences. With clear examples and powerful reflection prompts, Allison Schultz proves that the fearless willingness to engage in radical self-inquiry is the ONLY way to become an authentic leader." —**Liz Fosslien and Mollie West Duffy, co-authors of *No Hard Feelings* and *Big Feelings***

"In *The Art of Being Human at Work*, Allison Schultz provides a challenge to any would-be leader, namely: we can take a person, or a project, only as far as we have traveled ourselves. Accordingly, identifying, listening, examining, confronting, and dialoguing with the plethora of voices within that are laying claim to our choices is the first step toward responsible leadership and legitimate authority over others. Schultz's work is helpful to each of us in this summons to accountability." —**James Hollis, Ph.D., author of *Finding Meaning in the Second Half of Life* and *Living an Examined Life***

"*The Art of Being Human at Work* is a delightful, poignant, and wise spiritual friend. Allison invites us through urgent questioning to move from the superficial into what is tangling us up. What she calls radical inquiry is the essential, often uncomfortable, transformative process of facing one's own shadows, building community with others, to become who we already are. Get this book for yourself and your team!" —**Koshin Paley Ellison, Zen teacher and author of *Untangled: Walking the Eightfold Path to Clarity, Courage, and Compassion***

"Ali Schultz's understanding of the complex psychology of entrepreneurs is truly remarkable. I'm not sure if anyone has thought more deeply about the intricate psychological landscape that entrepreneurs and their leadership teams navigate. This book is a testament to her exceptional ability to connect with and understand entrepreneurs on their journey. Open any page and you will quickly feel recognized, understood, and skillfully guided toward wiser life choices by Ali. This book is an incredible gift to those who believe better humans make better leaders." —**Sebastian Ross, co-founder and Director of IESE School of Founders**

"If you've ever spent much time talking to Ali Schultz, you know that she just gets things on a level that few others do. These essays, like Ali, are deep and soulful and poetic. I frequently say to my clients, 'This would all be a lot easier if you didn't care!' This book is a valuable map for leaders who do care, who want to go beyond 'business as usual' and engage with what it means to be human (and humane) at work—with all the joy and pain that brings." —**Heather Jassy, executive coach and former SVP at Etsy**

"*The Art of Being Human at Work* is a compelling guide for entrepreneurs, founders, and CEOs looking to create successful, purposeful organizations while also focusing on their own personal growth. Schultz demonstrates how embracing discomfort, facing fears, and cultivating vulnerability can lead to a more authentic and courageous self, as well as foster the trust and communication that form the foundation of conscious leadership." —**Khe Hy, founder and CEO of RadReads**

"We are shaped by stories. In *The Art of Being Human at Work*, Allison Schultz gives us tools to understand the stories we carry and questions that lead us toward fulfillment. Both curious and kind, it approaches work as an invitation to be connected—to our communities and ourselves." —**Benjamin Perry, author of *Cry, Baby: Why Our Tears Matter***

"In my work with patients, I've often seen how hiding our true selves can lead to chronic stress, burnout, and a range of physical ailments. *The Art of Being Human at Work* offers a holistic approach to leadership, emphasizing the importance of self-care, mindfulness, and embodiment. Allison Schultz's wisdom and experience will guide you in creating a workplace where individuals feel seen, heard, and valued, ultimately leading to greater fulfillment and success for all. This is a must-read for every professional who wants to bring more compassion and authenticity into their daily work." —**Linnea Passaler, author of *Heal Your Nervous System***

"Right away, you get the sense that being more yourself and being a great leader are the same endeavor. Through provocative chapter headings, quotes that make you pause and close your eyes, and questions that pull at you to answer them, Ali helps you 'know thyself' and find the leader you want to be already inside yourself." —**Akshay Kapur, head of coaching at Automattic**

"Entrepreneurship has high-highs, low-lows, and everything in between. It's a rollercoaster ride for one's heart. These essays normalize the human experience every entrepreneur faces. Reboot's impact in entrepreneurs' lives over the past decade—with podcasts and free content that speaks right to the heart of the matter—is always timely and an essential accompaniment for the leader's journey." —**Brad Feld, partner and co-founder of Foundry**

"*The Art of Being Human at Work* gently reminds us that we're always in the never-quite-figured-out messiness in between order and mystery, in between the safety of what we know and the potential of what could be. Yet that's where growth happens, as long as we never stop the radical self-inquiry that helps us get to know and accept ourselves, helping us be more human and more ourselves at work and in life." —**Evgeny Shadchnev, author of *Startup CEO Succession***

"This book is for everyone who wants to become a better leader and a better person. People at all ages and stages of life will benefit from reading this book. The specific stories and essays organized into key leadership themes makes this book unique and practical. Allison integrates numerous quotes and resources that add even more value to her content. I will buy this book for my coaching clients at all levels. Since there is no finish line for "the art of being human," this is a book that is timeless. The shelf life has no expiration date." —**Jann E. Freed, PhD, author of *Breadcrumb Legacy: How Great Leaders Live a Life Worth Remembering* and *Leading with Wisdom: Sage Advice from 100 Experts***

"In these pages you will find yourself reading raw relatability with the rhythm of poetry and the pull of your favorite novel. Allison has compiled for us a collection of windows into understanding what it is to be a leader. This can be read from cover to cover or simply open to any page; inevitably you will find yourself less alone and with practical prompts to reflect on." —**Miriam Meima, CEO of the 2 Million Leaders Project**

"What a gift to be reminded that the work of being a leader cannot be collapsed into checklists and strategies, but rather involves our hearts and souls—the expansive wholeness of who we are. Ali's collection of essays invites the reader to go on a journey of uncovering one's fierce and tender self through incisive questions and deep-time wisdom." —**Chrystal Bell, executive coach**

"In this collection of smart essays, sprinkled with important questions to get you reflecting and scribbling, Ali takes us on a journey of exploration and self-discovery toward being more human at work. She's there as our honest guide, inviting us to figure out not only who we are as leaders, but who we are as humans. Helping us to show up in the fullness of our lives, find the courage we need, and lay a foundation of trust with others, this book is an essential compass for personal growth and development." —**Ian Sanders, storyteller, author, trainer, and coach**

 REBOOT®

hello@reboot.io

CREATIVE DIRECTOR: Saeah Wood
PRODUCTION AND EDITORIAL MANAGER: Amy Reed
EDITORIAL: Amy Reed, Terri Armstrong Welch, and Matthew Hoover
DESIGN: Ivica Jandrijević
AUTHOR PHOTO: Peggy Dyer

This book was made with love by humans and does not contain any AI generated content.

PAPERBACK ISBN: 979-8-9903452-0-1
E-BOOK ISBN: 979-8-9903452-1-8

 OTTERPINE

otterpine.com

The ART of
BEING
HUMAN
at WORK

ALLISON SCHULTZ

*Becoming a leader is synonymous with becoming yourself.
It is precisely that simple, and also that difficult.*

—Warren Bennis

The unexamined life is not worth living.

—Socrates

*And if you choose to live an unexamined life, please
don't take a job that involves other people.*

—Parker J. Palmer

*Imagine if we measured success by the amount
of safety people felt in our presence.*

—Jonathan Louis Dent

I scarcely know where to begin, but love is always a safe place.

—Emily Dickinson

To the emerging leader: may you trust that the process of becoming more *you* leads to the fortitude, resolve, grace, and magic on the roller coaster of life.

This book is dedicated to your heart.

CONTENTS

PART IV
EMBRACING CHANGE

PART V
LAYING A FOUNDATION OF TRUST

PART VI
EMBODIED LEADERSHIP

FOREWORD

The Struggle to Be Human
By Jerry Colonna

Rumi taught that the experience of being human is like a guesthouse where we should welcome "a joy, a depression, a meanness" as an "unexpected visitor." As true as Rumi's teaching is, the welcoming of it all can be quite a struggle. This being human is hard.

We see this difficulty in the ways folks try to mitigate the struggle by obsessing over the practical realities of leading and growing up. We see the efforts to lessen the difficult tasks of leading, managing, and adulting by fixating on the *how* of leadership. And, as important as such efforts are—and to be clear, they are important—learning the skills of managing does little to relieve the struggle of being a fully human leader.

And so we see, time and again, folks turning to trendy hacks to bypass and shortcut their way to relief. They'll turn to age-old proven techniques for radical self-inquiry—practices like journaling or meditation, for example—in an attempt to quickly fix their way to relief. They'll consume 'shrooms or perform superficial versions of other forms of ancient wisdom without the accompanying insight necessary to further their development into adulthood. Unfortunately, rather than using these practices as entry points into real radical self-inquiry, what often happens is that they're used to bypass the struggle and, more importantly, the work it takes to grow into our full selves.

I think now of the young man who came up to me recently at a book signing. "How can I be fully actualized?" he tenderly asked me, his eyes welling up. I was struck by the incongruity of his simple, somewhat intellectual question and the felt sense that behind his question was a dull ache of self-dissatisfaction.

"Tell me more about your question," I responded, leaning in a bit so I could both hear and sense him better. All I really knew at that moment was that he was in his twenties and came from a family of very successful parents and grandparents. From our brief conversations prior to this moment, I knew he didn't want to screw up the legacy he'd inherited—a legacy of both success and wealth. "Tell me more about what needs to be actualized," I continued.

He spoke about all the various life hacks he'd been reading and hearing about. Podcasts and books that spoke reverently of the ways one could optimize one's sleep, fight inflammation, meditate away one's anxieties, or even medicate one's way past the dull ache of self-dissatisfaction. "'Shrooms and journaling," I imagined him wishing me to advise. "Take two and call me in the morning."

Instead, I pressed him in a different way. "Tell me what needs to be made better, made whole, what might be in need of actualization," I said, wary of the proclivity of so many to bypass the work necessary to finally feel that they belong. His tears flowed more freely now. "What if you're already actualized?" I asked. His shoulders, which had been close to his ears, let themselves down and his heart seemed to slow.

He handed me a copy of my book *Reunion* for me to sign. On the blank page near the front, I wrote his name and added "Remember...you're already actualized. You always have been. Love, Jerry."

What if you're already actualized? How would that change your experience in this life you have?

In this wonderful collected work, these are the types of questions that Ali challenges each of us to contemplate. Reflect on, struggle through, wrestle with, and, in an act of deep self-compassion, bear witness to instead of skipping to the very end.

Carl Jung famously said that the whole person isn't merely one who has walked with God but one who has also wrestled with the devil. This wrestling is the pre-work necessary to enjoy the art of becoming and being a fully actualized, fully whole human—in the workplace and beyond. Even though it feels so hard, this wrestling is a form of self-compassion. For that is the essence of compassion: to be with the feelings, no matter the challenge, and to welcome them all in. In this way, we turn the struggle into an art by bearing witness to it all.

This is, to me, the best part of *The Art of Being Human at Work*. Indeed, it is the meditative aspect of this collection of short but powerful essays that makes it so effective. You are now able to read these meditations, not over the course of years as they were first published, but as a whole. And in this way you can see Ali's art at work, how she circles around the essence of being human, of being with the human part of ourselves. The result is a guidebook that shows—rather than tells—how one might create the space of our humanity while preserving such space for those whom we are privileged to lead—so they may be their human selves as well. Think of this book as an accompaniment, and think of Ali as your companion, on this journey into your own humanity.

Ali and I, as well as our colleagues at Reboot, are famously known for the tears we can invoke. As often as not, they flow from the simple but powerful questions we often ask of ourselves and of those with whom we work. "How are you?" we ask, not as a throwaway line but as an empathetic bridge—one heart connecting to another. How are you and, more importantly, how has your wish to love and be loved, to feel safe, and to belong motivated your frantic push to be the best leader and the best adult you can be? And further, how has that wish led you to a whole series of self-defeating thoughts and actions? Hanging around Reboot folks, one can expect tears to flow. And those tears flow mostly because our simple but hard questions create space for that human to be seen, held, and respected.

For more than ten years, Ali has not only been the voice of Reboot but the voice of those who struggle with the art of being human. From organizing our very first bootcamp—where it was evident that this way of coaching, of releasing people from the self-imposed burden of stories they hold about who they should be—to the release of this collection of her best writing, Ali continues to lead us in making sense of our broken-open hearts. For all that time, she has given voice to and chronicled the part of being human that is too often overlooked and, therefore, bypassed in a vain attempt to ward off the terrors of leadership. The resulting dehumanization of ourselves and our colleagues is the consequence of valuing output over people in order to ignore the devil instead of wrestling with it.

Ali resists the temptation to fix, preferring instead to take the coach's stance of bearing witness while ever mindful of her own journeys and struggles. She offers her own radical self-inquiry in service to, and in support of, your journey.

Perhaps this is the ultimate expression of the art of being human: to acknowledge our own struggle while staying connected to the struggles of others. In this way, as with so many other bits of wisdom from elders such as Rumi, the art is a function of the practice. The art of being human then, is the practice of welcoming it all in, and in doing so, finally seeing that you've been human all along.

INTRODUCTION

*Better leaders are better humans and better
humans are better leaders. Leadership lessons then,
at their core, are lessons in humanity.*

—Jerry Colonna

The inner landscape of an entrepreneur is where inspiration and the practical-tactical meet the realities of building a business. There are ups and downs, and some quick turns—much like a roller coaster. It's a ride that we opt in to (though, sometimes we forget that it's a *choice*)—one that sometimes makes us feel like we're soaring, and at other times makes our stomach churn.

Most twists and turns are beyond our control. The pandemic especially has taught us that. The key to riding this roller coaster well is finding a way to metabolize the ups and downs as they occur.

For many people, founding and running a business (or working at a scaling startup) puts life on full throttle. Big sacrifices are made in the name of mission statements and promises of big returns that often take a toll on our health, our relationships, and our mental well-being. When we sign up for this entrepreneurial roller coaster, there's as much foreboding as excitement: it's a wild ride in this work/life amusement park as we discover our own twists and turns.

When you boarded the roller coaster of entrepreneurship, what is it that you signed up for? What did you leave behind? What did you assume about the ride you chose? How did your assumptions and beliefs about work influence your choice? Looking at things *now*: What or how might you choose differently?

What would be different if you approached your work choices from a place grounded in a sense of self-worth? How many of the choices made around your job, company, or career are based on a belief that you are not enough or not valuable outside of your accomplishments and bank accounts?

How we consider work within the scope of our whole life is a perspective that can take us off the roller coaster.

Enter: Transformational Coaching

Coaching clients come to Reboot with a varied set of pain points such as bullying executives, misbehaving board members, CEOs struggling to step away from the day-to-day as the company scales, imposter syndrome, and challenges with delegation and trust. Many of these are people issues, as much as they have practical-tactical components. Many of these are part and parcel of the growing pains encountered as a company grows and the leader grows—or is forced to grow—into their role.

In most cases simply knowing *what* to do only solves half the problem due to the human dynamics at play in any situation. The human factors make for a complexity that often isn't touched by simply applying best practices, new systems, and methodologies. Each scenario is a unique case that requires a sensitivity to nuance because of what's really happening at the human level. This is where the *how* you do it comes in.

As coaches, we know it takes both practical skills (operational know-how) and radical self-inquiry to address most issues fully. When it comes to success in building/running/leading a business, you can't have one without the other. Radical self-inquiry on its own can skew towards aloofness and turn you into the proverbial philosopher on a log. Practical skills only may deny the human experience, the heart and the humanity of what it means to lead an organization. And if you don't know yourself, especially as a leader, you're a risk and a potential danger to your team and organization.

Practical skills + radical self-inquiry: both are necessary parts of what it takes to grow, build, and sustain a great company.

Many clients come to us essentially to learn how to lead. Their often anxiety-driven belief is that leading is some mysterious art that they alone were never taught. If they could just figure out how to do the job then they'll feel better, they think.

We believe the opposite is true. That is, if you can learn to manage your psyche, your anxieties, and the nearly constant sensation of failing, then you can be a leader. And the leader who emerges is essentially authentic and trustworthy.

This belief is at the heart of the Reboot formula:

**PRACTICAL SKILLS + RADICAL SELF-INQUIRY
+ SHARED EXPERIENCES =
GREATER RESILIENCY + ENHANCED LEADERSHIP**

This process undergirds everything we do—and it is the core theme of the essays you will read in this book. We believe that helping clients develop the managerial skills necessary to do the job is important but not enough to create the transformation they are seeking. To be an authentic leader, they must also cultivate a fearless willingness to look deeply through self-inquiry.

This path of radical self-inquiry leads us to discover what we most want in our lives, our authentic purpose, that which is in line with our most deeply held values. Along the way, we begin to see new choices emerging: opportunities to reframe, refine, and revise our mental models that lead to new behavioral options.

As Reboot co-founder Jerry Colonna writes in his book *Reboot: Leadership and the Art of Growing Up*:

> The most challenging piece of the formula—indeed, the most important—is this notion of radically inquiring within. I define it as the process by which self-deception becomes so skillfully and compassionately exposed that there's no mask that can hide us anymore. The notion is to recognize that if things are not okay, if you're struggling, you stop pretending and allow yourself to get help. Even more, it's the process by which you work hard to know yourself—your strengths, your struggles, your true intentions, your true motivations, the characteristics of the character known as "you." The you behind the masks, the stories, the protective but no longer useful belief systems that have been presented for so long as the "you" you'd like everyone to see.

For an organization to fully self-actualize requires that everyone in the organization self-actualize. You can't have one without the other. Being part of an organization implies that you cannot do it alone. Coming together towards an organizational goal means you have to communicate in order to coordinate action. All communication comes from a deep set of beliefs and values, and if you are unaware of what those are and are not living from them (as well as respecting others' beliefs and values) you cannot create a nonviolent or humane workplace.

Startups and non-startup-y organizations can be turbulent places, but they don't have to be. The promise is that they're better than the corporate or cubicled alternative, and yet much happens when we're scaling fast at the organizational level. It pays to be conscious about not only *what* we're doing but *how* we're doing it. On the path to doing something amazing, an early reflex is to define ourselves by what we're *not* going to be. But we have to be mindful of what we are creating, and set out intentions for what's possible.

At Reboot, we know that **Better Humans Make Better Leaders** and **Better Leaders Make More Humane Workplaces**. We believe that work can be the way we achieve our fullest selves.

Why the Art of Being Human at Work?

The word *art* denotes a feeling. It's something books can't contain in bulleted lists and checklists. There's not enough room in a checklist for art to happen. We can know every best practice and follow every checklist, but we will also be with ourselves along the way, the whole time. Unless we execute like a robot, we feel each moment and every bullet point in the relational spaces that make up *work*.

Likewise, we're required to feel our way through to crafting our own life, our own playbook, according to our heart.

Art and feeling can't be hacked or engineered. The same goes for the best kind of leadership: you must bring together self-awareness, practical-tactical know-how, intuition and instinct, and a lot of people skills. People, unlike software, require soft skills to be in tip-top shape: listening, asking open-ended questions, being clear on what's yours and what's theirs, knowing which tendencies we all bring to the table that get in our own way of being clear, leading well, and leading by example.

The essays in this book have been curated to explore this art of leadership, selected from over ten years of newsletters and blog posts on Reboot's website. Originally written to accompany our podcast, they have been adapted to stand alone and organized based on many of the core themes we encounter again and again with our clients. You can read the book sequentially or hop around based on what calls to you. How you read this book, like your leadership journey, is up to you. More than anything, our hope is that these essays will be tools of inspiration and introspection. Consider moving through the book slowly, letting each essay have time to settle, perhaps using it as a prompt for your own writing or journaling—that is, your own radical self-inquiry. In this way, this book can be a source of daily meditation on the intersection of life and work.

This book is for anyone who works in startups or scaleups—from solopreneurs to heads of nonprofits to CEOs of Fortune 500 companies, and the people who invest in them. To all who want to do the deep work of becoming a better leader to create a more humane workplace and a better world, let this book be a resource to help guide you to your own authentic life.

We at Reboot believe that work does not have to destroy us. Work can be the way in which we achieve our fullest selves. Welcome to our conversation around life and work. We're so glad you're here.

Part I

MAKING PEACE WITH YOUR SHADOWS

WHY TRACKING YOUR SHADOW IS ESSENTIAL TO BEING A LEADER (AND A BETTER HUMAN)

The concept of the shadow self was coined by psychoanalyst Carl Jung to describe the parts of our psyches that we repress or choose not to acknowledge—in other words, our emotional blind spots. Shadow work is the practice of understanding the parts of self you deny or are not conscious of. These denied, unprocessed, or unintegrated parts of us show up in ways that are not always tidy for the other humans we get to work with. Without fully examining our own personal baggage, our own unexamined stuff may start coming out sideways, which lends itself to ask...

> What drives us to do what we do?

> Why do good people do bad things?

> What is our relationship with power and status?

and...

How Do We Recognize Our Shadow?

Shadow shows up when we have unresolved issues about our beliefs and relationship to ourselves. It's the part of us that abides by the maxim "it's better to be small and inauthentic than emotionally crushed." It wants to keep us safe but ultimately limits our full expression.

Shadows are cast by our unsorted psychological baggage. This includes what we've left unfinished, stuffed under the rug, locked in our inner closets out of shame, or any of the other unresolved issues we tote along with us, inside us, every day.

Author, educator, and founder of the Center for Courage and Renewal Parker J. Palmer notes in his book *Let Your Life Speak* that the following five aspects of our personality and experience of being human are capable of casting shadows in our lives and for those in it:

> Insecurity about identity and self-worth
> The belief that the world is a hostile place
> Functional atheism (the belief that ultimate responsibility for everything rests with us)
> Fears (especially of chaos and uncertainty)
> Denial of death and fear of failure

This is the importance of shadow work: if we don't work on our stuff, our stuff will work on us. It will work on us when even our best intentions are to have an amazing life. And it will show up everywhere, projecting its own reality in front of us like a bad movie—or perhaps recurring situations we keep finding ourselves in—until it is brought to light. Once we see it and learn how it operates, we can recognize it when it shows up.

Reclaiming what's in shadow brings those pieces of you back into wholeness. It allows you to see the projection and walk out of that theater into your more dimensional life. It allows you to harness your potential more effectively. Embracing what's shadowed helps you find a tender love for yourself, warts and all.

Unchecked shadow shows up in infidelity, sexual misconduct, fiscal irresponsibility, misuse of power, and putting on a face for the crowd that's different from the life you experience with those closest to you. What's called for in our work is for all that makes us human—the vulnerability, the self-inquiry, our true voice. How we do this with ourselves shows up in our work and our ability to be present with those we are called to serve. The work starts with self, first.

How do we go about doing the work to save ourselves from ourselves, and subsequently save those around us from the collateral damage that results from acting out from our shadow and leading an unexamined life? This is the question to circumambulate in our own hearts. If you're not doing your own work—your inner work—you're not living a congruent life. (In other words, you're not becoming fully you.) And your work in life ripples out from that place of incongruency.

In *The Wisdom of the Desert: Sayings from the Desert Fathers of the Fourth Century*, theologian and poet Thomas Merton tells us: "What can we gain by sailing to the moon if we are not able to cross the abyss that separates us from ourselves? This is the most important of all voyages of discovery, and without it all the rest are not only useless but disastrous."

A LA MODE

With a little more care, a little more courage, and, above all, a little more soul, our lives can be so easily discovered and celebrated in work, and not, as now, squandered and lost in its shadow.

—David Whyte

We learn much about work from our parents. For me, the Midwestern work ethic is in my bones. Where I come from, however, work was what you did to pay the bills even if that meant that your soul suffered in the process. While I know how and when to work hard, to sweat and get my hands in the dirt, and am grateful for that grit and gumption, I'm a renegade when it comes to the other principles about work that I learned from watching those in my lineage. I know I'm not alone in that detour from tradition.

I'm not sure my folks thought much about setting their own vision of success and working towards that, or about aligning their purpose with their income-generating work in the world, or about becoming the adult they wanted to be and building the company they wanted to work for. But I did, and still do. I just couldn't sacrifice the deepest truth of my being or martyr the dreams stirring in me in order to make a living—not for long, anyway. (My soul withers just thinking about it.)

One of my favorite lines about relating to work is from Willy Wonka: "Invention, my dear friends, is 93% perspiration, 6% electricity, 4% evaporation, and 2% butterscotch ripple." It's playful. It's fun. It captures the magic of combining elements seen and unseen, the sweat, the energy, and the flavor that persists at the end of it all.

When you play with what you love as opposed to doing it the way everyone else is doing it, you're in charge of all that goes into your invention, your business. That includes your growth, your less-than-delicious experiments, and all the juicy nuggets along the way. There's a sweetness to that entire process that's worth celebrating more often than we do. So let's start here:

> How do you acknowledge your successes?

> What have you accomplished in the past three months? The past year? Up until this point in your life?

> How have you grown as a person?

> What can you celebrate *right now*?

We're so glad you're here to share the deeper inquiries around work and all that we bring to it as humans looking for purpose and meaning. Starting from a place of celebration of who we are and what we've already accomplished can set the stage for a joyful journey of growth for a lifetime.

OUR INHERITANCE, OUR LEGACY

Our first experiences in life shape so much about the selves we become and are always becoming. From our first moments in the womb, we're constantly absorbing information about our world and making sense of who we are from our parents. Under their influence and care, we form our identity and ideas about the world. We form beliefs about who we are, what it means to be human, how to belong, what it takes to be loved and to love, what emotions mean, how god works (or doesn't), and how we feel about money—all greatly influenced by our upbringing, whether we like it or not.

The apple doesn't fall far from the tree, often in ways that we admit only reluctantly. Yet when we look back over who imprinted us and how we are now, it's a hard realization to deny. Sometimes we have to break our idealized image of our perfect parental units, or perhaps one of our parental figures. But our parents are humans too, who were raised by their own parents, who were likely less than perfect. And on it goes. This isn't spirituality. It doesn't matter if you're an atheist, side with the stoics, make a pilgrimage to Burning Man, or abide by any other scripture in the global religio-philosophical cannon. This is all part of being human.

As we emerge into our lives as vulnerable little humans, we are like impressionable clay—or a freshly set up developmental environment, ready for new code in the human way to be. From our parental units we compile and interpret all that new information flooding our experience, which we then log as programs to run when we need it.

The stories that live inside us, wired by our neural nets, carry our uniquely tailored maps of the world. These include the positive as well as the negative feelings and meanings about events that happened as they are recorded in our memories. Some have more charge than others and are noted as such out of our body's penchant for self-preservation. Until we do some inner housecleaning later in life to look at what we've packed along with us, we'll stick in the same cycles before we can re-sort it all and decide what we would (really, really, really) like.

I remember once sitting in my therapist's office, responding to a series of questions he asked about memories I had growing up: "Who took care of you when you were sick? What would they do for you? Who would you run to if you were hurt? Who would play with you, and how? When did you feel cared for? Did your parents ever get angry? What was that like...?"

I answered and then stood back and took a meta stance on my responses. I could feel how certain moments, and my view of them as a whole, had shaped my current experience. It was unnerving. At the end of the session, my therapist asked curiously, "Can you see how these experiences impacted you?" Once again, I was amazed by how much our formidable years are, well, formidable.

While I was there to explore moving forward with my significant other in new choreography, I couldn't get to the new territory without really seeing how the old stuff was playing out in my current rendition of things—and how it was all connected to the meanings I made during childhood. So often in our daily lives, the past is present so much so that it's like the movie *Groundhog Day*, as we live out the same patterns programmed into us from the imprints at the various stages of our human development.

Both denying that fact and being attached to it keep us from meeting life fully. We live in the shadows of our parents, rebel against them in a polarizing attempt to not be like them. Or we hold the wounds from our past close to our chest, on our sleeve, and knit into our identity in a way that leaves us small and living for and in the past. Getting a clear view of what our parental imprints are and how they're showing up in our lives is a key exercise to being able to change and to tread into new, uncharted territory in our map of experience.

In his book *The Middle Passage: From Misery to Meaning in Midlife*, Jungian analyst James Hollis writes that after childhood, we enter our first adulthood starting at age twelve until age forty. (Forty-ish is about the stage of midlife.) If we choose to progress in our lives, we enter a second adulthood around age forty until old age. This is where a truer self emerges from the shadows and steps into their life differently. Folks who don't move into the second phase of adulthood live unlived lives. This is because, as Hollis puts it, "the first adulthood is…full of blunders, shyness, inhibitions, mistaken assumptions, and always, the silent rolling of the tapes of childhood."

If you're reading this, I'd wager that you're not someone vying for an *unlived* life. For most of us ambitious types, that's what we fear most, right? We wanna suck the marrow out of our one wild and precious life. So, how do we become ourselves, minus the silent rolling tapes of childhood? Moreover, how do we prevent these childhood tapes from playing a big role in our businesses and companies?

While our histories repeat themselves, these historical imperatives aren't necessarily imperative. Cue Carl Jung: "I am not what has happened to me. I am what I choose to become." Or, as Jerry points out, "The self-inquiry process asks Who am I? and What am I working with here?" Our work is to take what happened to us and shape our own self, consciously growing beyond the imprints of our historics.

Once you become aware of these patterns, you can notice where they show up, how they show up, and what makes them come alive—and you can give yourself the space to choose something different. You can get curious and ask yourself these questions:

> What are these things I'm doing and why?

> Where do they come from?

> When did they first show up?

> What do they remind me of?

> How are my childhood imprints and beliefs showing up right now?

> What do my lineage and family history tell me about what I am experiencing now?

> What ties to these invisible things may be holding me back?

And the most important question of all:

> What do I want?

For Hollis, the questions that push us into real adulthood in the second half of life shift from How do I survive in this world I landed in? to Who, apart from the roles I play, am I? What does the soul ask of me? Do I have the wherewithal to shift course, to deconstruct my painfully achieved identity, risking failure, marginalization, and loss of collective approval?

To get there, which Hollis asserts is "no small task," we need to tend to the unsorted baggage of our lives.

In doing so, we can heal the wounds in our own hearts, lifting a burden from the next generation.

What Do You Know about Your Family History? How Can That Empower Your Leadership and Purpose?

The ancestral math tells us that for you to be alive today from twelve previous generations, you needed over four thousand ancestors over the past four hundred years to come before you. Consider the span of history of your people for a moment. Where did they come from? What has happened over the past four hundred years? What did they survive? How much sadness was there? How much heartbreak? How much joy? What were the battles and difficulties, the casualties, and inner prisons? What was the hope they had for the future? If you think and feel into what you know from the range of emotion and experience from your life to date, compound that by over four thousand relatives' experiences. So much of that history still pulses in you, here and now.

You may be wondering: What does my family tree have to do with my company? I can tell you that we see threads of this present in many different clients. The entrepreneur whose business is going great, yet he is anxious that "it's all going to go away." One person's seeming inability to find a lasting romantic relationship. The person who at her core feels alone, terrified, and sad despite a very good life full of purpose—and a business that's doing well. Or the entrepreneur who lives out his father's patterns without realizing it.

And yet, while the echoes of the past might be reverberating for you now, these are not necessarily your burdens to carry. By healing what's showing up from unresolved moments in previous generations, we stop the pain, the suffering, and unconscious loyalties we maintain to stay connected to those who came before us. The past that lives out in our current lives, if we catch it and course-correct, relieves future generations from reliving that pattern too.

What do you know about your family tree? Who are the shoulders on which you stand? What were their stories, their fears, their losses, their hopes, their loves? What do they want most for you?

If we can connect to our family histories in a more conscious way, sometimes the family connection can feel less like a burden and more like a resource.

LOOKING ASKEW

The shadow is often referred to as a black bag that you drag behind yourself, filled with all the things that you haven't been able to consciously look at for a variety of reasons: you weren't ready to, you couldn't, it was too much, etc. And yet, wherever you go, there it is—behind you in the dark.

(I must tell you about the dream I had the night before sitting down to write this essay. It involved me getting ready to hop on a flight and realizing that the luggage I had was not carry-on size. I opened this big black suitcase and tried to repack it so I could bring it on the plane and get where I wanted to go. As I reevaluated the contents of the black bag, my parents appeared and I handed them back things I didn't need as I was sorting through what to repack. Talk about symbolism!)

Ah, shadow.

Years ago, before I began a deep dive with my first coach and mentor, she asked me: "Are you willing to look at the shadow side of you? The part of you that doesn't want you to do all that you aspire to do? Are you willing to see, listen to, and look directly at anything in you that is wanting to hold you back? And what might be the greatest potential gift in doing that?"

I had little idea what this meant. The thought of looking at something I hadn't even known about seemed terrifying, quite honestly.

At that point, my mind raced a bit: Why hadn't I seen this shadow thing before? What was I going to find? Looking at this seemingly terrifying, potent dark thing was going to be a gift? What the... ?!

She explained that shadow is that part of us that tells us it's better to be small and inauthentic than emotionally crushed. The greatest potential gift of looking at that square in the face still seemed to me a bit like eating an entire box of Cracker Jacks only to be left with a gut ache and a lame-ass prize. In other words, way more trouble that it was worth. But I trusted her, and I was willing to do what it took to change, and therein began my exploration of the dark.

The dark side wasn't as terrifying as part of me had imagined. I met and got reacquainted with stuff from childhood. The young reasonings I used to try and make sense of those events were still running in the background cycles of my experience, which created a current perception of reality that was operating from an old map. And that old map was projecting old things that were not going to get me where I aspired to be. In fact, they were getting in the way.

What lies in our shadow is a projection of reality, but not reality itself. When these projections are left unquestioned or not brought to light and examined, we begin to believe them as truth. Yet our version of reality is often quite subjective—more subjective than our *view* of it can often seem. Shadow work helps us see ourselves, our actions, our motivations, and our behaviors more clearly.

Through my initial work, as I found more clarity, it was like I was shifting from a fragmented camera obscura projection of reality to the direct experience in the dimensions of embodied life. Once the old maps of distorted images stopped running as background cycles, more of my resources showed up for myself, my work, my relationships, and my play. With that energy freed up, I found a refreshing and renewed sense of life itself.

"How you choose to interact with the opposing forces within you will determine your life. Starve one or the other, or guide them both," says an old Cherokee story. Learning to work with shadow could be one of the most liberating things you can do in your relationships—with yourself, your work, and your intimate friends and partners—leading you towards living more fully in alignment with your purpose.

Know what the most beautiful part is? When it comes to shadow work, your medicine is always right in front of you. What you create tells you something potent about how what's in the black bag may be showing up for you. It's good to get curious, look askew, and investigate what's playing on the screen from behind you in the dark. Only then can you get the full 360-degree view, and only then can you make fully empowered choices about where you're going.

PART AND PARCEL

A mentor of mine once told me that we are many ages showing up at any given moment, regardless of our chronological age. Many "parts" within our psyche make up who we think we are. They could have developed as early as infancy or during our formative years. Really any moment from any age in our timeline of life experiences can get logged into our neurological wiring so we don't forget. As these new neural pathways form, they are occasionally of such importance to "us" that they get cemented in and become harder to change. These are parts that make up our core beliefs about our identity, and they are always present in ways we may or may not be fully aware of.*

Parts form inside us as we live through moments with big feelings—such as that time no one came to soothe us when we were a few months old, or our first big birthday party at age three, or when our parents divorced at age seven. We weave meaning into these feelings and events, and the memories freeze in time and stop developing. This makes it hard to keep all our parts on the same track as we move forward in life, since they don't evolve with our chronological age as we grow older. If you ever said to yourself, "On the one hand I think/feel/want this, but on the other hand I think/feel/want this," you know that a few parts of you are showing up with a few differing desires, points of view, and interests in mind.

---

* Parts work comes from many places historically, and is most commonly known in Internal Family Systems (IFS) work by Richard Schwartz. I learned about parts work from Carl Buchheit at NLP Marin.

We have all done this at various times, growing up as humans. Something happened at a much younger age about which we made a decision consciously or unconsciously, and that program runs until we become aware of it in our much older life. That often means we may have many, many programs running our present lives that are operating out of conclusions we reached in the past. When this happens, and we start noticing them, we can find ourselves having experiences that feel eerily familiar, over and over again.

Take for example a five-year-old who arrives at a new school in a new part of town, awkward as the new kid and a bit shy, desperately wanting to be liked, but having a rough go of fitting in with the new crowd. As an adult, he becomes a well-connected, extroverted person, still driven by the longing to be liked. In general, there's nothing problematic about this. However, when this tendency is driven by a fear of not fitting in (experiencing what happened when he was a five-year-old all over again) it can become an important feeling to manage and the default way in which he orients his life, guiding how he shows up and interacts with people, including those at his company.

Another example: A woman who grew up with an alcoholic father and who vowed to herself at a young age to never be like him. She keeps her sh*t together, is efficient, and accomplishes much in her young career. All good things, right? But there's still a little girl in there who, prior to determining to not be like her father, was sad, angry, hurt, and staving off anyone or anything that would fall short and disappoint. So, she does everything herself and has a hard time delegating.

One can think of these parts as our psyche's many façades or neurological wire-sets, imprinted from our various ages still living out their worldview. When parts of us are active, as in the examples above, it's as if the five-year-old (or whatever age) self is operating in their adult-sized body. These younger parts need to be cared for and tended to if we're to become an adult committed to making conscious choices for ourselves.

How can we stride forth with more authenticity, with all our parts on board with what we want? How can we ensure that our wise, adult self is the primary consciousness of our mature adult lives?

The important thing to remember is that these parts of ourselves are like young and confused children who have our best interests in mind (according to their youthful understandings). They have made sense of the world from a place of great duty in service to us, so we don't do X, Y, or Z again; or end up like so-and-so; or avoid feeling (insert intense set of emotions here). Sometimes these parts take on a responsibility that isn't theirs, or they create loyalties to others to make someone else's life better. They take on jobs that no child can ever solve. These parts of ourselves were perhaps at one time wounded or worried and have made decisions to ensure our lovability, safety, and belonging. These neural wires burned into our psyche in the past operate fast to protect us even to this day.

Once you uncover one of these parts of yourself, you can turn to it as if it really is a child and address what it needs, almost literally, in your mind's eye. When you have compassion for your "little ones" from your current place in the chronological timeline in your life, you can reassure them, love them, and remind them that they are safe, everything is A-OK. You can quell the fear lodged in that imprinted neurological wiring. Thank them for their concern, and remind them of what you've survived to date and how the world is now (i.e., how good things are that they don't have to believe so strongly anymore whatever it is that they are holding on to). You can put that little part right beside you as you go through life (in the copilot's seat, but not in the driver's seat).

Sometimes these parts of ourselves are close to our loyal soldiers (more about loyal soldiers in the essay "Where Your Loyalties Lie" on page 40), which we often find when we do some shadow work.

Mostly, they need an update on the current state of the union (you!) and a reminder that they aren't the primary self responsible for making decisions anymore. Once your parts are heard and seen, they can finally relax and let grown-up you take the reins. This is part and parcel of self-compassion.

HITTING THE WALL

Most of us have two lives. The life we live, and the unlived life within us. Between the two stands Resistance.

—Steven Pressfield

I can't help but notice that Steven Pressfield refers to Resistance with a capital R. It's inevitable and relentless. Resistance is something we all work with, whether we're aware of it or not, as we grow (or not) into our lives. When it comes to living out what we want most and doing our work—the work we are here to do, the person we are here to become—resistance is the wall between where we are and where we'd like to be.

If I don't explore my resistance, I end up living a contained life and find myself bound in that container (perhaps steeping in some self-loathing), despite wanting to leave it behind. I will not do what I say I long to do, or I may never change into what I most want to become. This may look and feel like keeping my best gifts and potency swaddled under wraps, or struggling to break free of them. The task, for ourselves, is to become aware of what our resistance looks like when it shows up, know how to handle it, and not let it get in the way of what we want most.

Resistance is often a good sign. It's a signal that we're coming close to something important. The bigger the importance, the bigger the resistance. Putting it another way, the closer we get to something we want or something deeply important to our psyche in terms of belief and identity, resistance will often show up in a variety of sly forms—from denial or intellectualization to cancelling a therapy session at the last minute or getting too busy to see your coach, mentor, new date, doctor, etc.

We all do it. We all have a wall (or a labyrinthine series of them) within ourselves. Placed there by early conditioning and self-preservation, it's made of resistance. Some of us have a locked room, within locked a room, within a locked room. And the most locked room of all is the room we deny exists. "What room? I don't see any rooms." (Or another favorite remark of resistance: "There's no such thing as the unconscious!")

When we hit the wall, resistance shows up. Resistance creates a blind spot so that we can't even see what's happening for us. Sometimes it doesn't want us to be even mildly suspect of our inner stuff that's lurking. (Insert denial. Insert avoidance. Insert rationalizations and intellectualizations.) We can't even see it for ourselves, although sometimes a dear friend or colleague can help us find a way through so we are not stopped by the wall.

What makes the wall of resistance so halting? How can we not talk ourselves out of/over it? Answer: Feelings! What you'll often find is that the deeper the resistance, the deeper the pain. This wall or labyrinthine series of walls we have inside ourselves was solidified to keep that deeply wounded part of us safe.

Working with resistance is a delicate thing. As Parker Palmer writes in *Let Your Life Speak*, "the soul is a shy, wild creature." You have to build rapport with it, sit on the sidelines with it, and be on its side to see what it has to say. You can't go talkin' straight to it, for the more you go up against it, the stronger it gets. Most often, resistance is rooted in a delusional statement or belief. Once you recognize and articulate what that is, you can see what's really happening for you. When you lean into your resistance in that way, you can then choose and shift into a more fluid space or state of mind.

Moving through and working with resistance requires some radical self-inquiry, which as Jerry describes it is "The process by which self-deception becomes so skillfully and compassionately exposed that there's no mask that can hide us anymore." Here, we can begin to see our blind spots.

What does your resistance look like? What are the thoughts and feelings that circle around when it is present? How does it feel in your body? What are you really feeling emotionally?

While resistance never leaves us alone entirely, we can work with it so it doesn't work us over. And once we notice its presence, we can separate ourselves from it, and in that space choose something else. When we can get in touch with what lies beyond the wall of resistance, what keeps us contained, we move into a truer part of ourselves. I am reminded of author Anaïs Nin's words, "And then the day came, when the risk to remain tight in a bud was more painful than the risk it took to blossom."

FATE AND DESTINY

I am not what has happened to me, I am what I choose to become.

—Carl Jung

The four weeks before my grandfather died were filled with conversations among family members. One afternoon while he was still in the hospital, he shared an observation with my aunt Randy. Gratefully reflecting on the arc of his life he said, "Who knew that two kids who had nothing, zero, would have what we have today. Back then, I couldn't have imagined I would have had the life I had, as much as we have now, and the family that we raised, and how successful our grandkids would be."

My grandparents came from families that had few material things and even less emotional support, but they came together and made a more than decent life for themselves and their family. They accepted their fate and moved well beyond its limitations; they were deeply imprinted by the circumstances they were born into. Their story is part of my story. It's something I can look back on and honor. Yet the specific fate I was squeezed out into from the womb is different than theirs, and my life's trajectory is my own. There is a difference between fate and destiny.

The facts of where you were born, when you were born, your physical body, who you were born to, and what lineages run in your veins are all part of your fate. Fate encompasses the things that were given to us, both advantages and limitations. Destiny, though, is our potential. It's what calls to us or tries to live through us. Once we land in this world with the hand of cards fate dealt us, what we do with those circumstances is how we make our destiny.

In a sense, the question posed by fate and destiny is, Do we create our lives, or does life create us? We are free to choose what we would like and follow what is moving through us. But in the space between fate and destiny is a catch point where we must tease out the imprints that keep us struggling to move forward as we'd desire, continually getting caught in an undertow from the past, and what is our authentic journey, moving freely into new territory. Sometimes even the decisions we think we're making freely are bound to a past. As Jung noted, "Until you make the unconscious conscious, it will direct your life and you will call it fate."

The key is to become aware of the sources of the repetitions we find ourselves in—the ones that hold us back, like the thoughts and inner warnings that sound like our parents' voices, not our own inner compass. It is then within those catch points that we can recognize what reactions and impulses feel familiar from the past and may be influencing our current decisions or actions—versus allowing us to be fully aligned within ourselves and move into a fresh newness of where we'd really like to be.

What and how are those invisible things ruling our lives? How do we get ahead of that to allow what's moving through us in this lifetime to move through freely, unbound by repetitions of history?

James Hollis writes in his book *Hauntings: Dispelling the Ghosts Who Run Our Lives*, "We are not our history; ultimately, we are what wishes to enter the world through us, though to underestimate the power of that history as an invisible player in the choices of our daily life is a grave error."

Perhaps the gift of radical self-inquiry is this: we can become conscious of the unconscious patterns and sabotaging snares that would otherwise stand in the way of glimpsing and seizing our destiny. Radical self-inquiry is deep work at the edge of the past and where your destiny is emerging. This work is much more than just a list of your strengths and weaknesses.

To love our fate is to understand in a meta-sense that we chose the starting position of life so that we could learn what we came here to learn. Destiny is the fulfillment of that lesson. That's radical self-inquiry and radical self-responsibility, a golden lesson in itself.

Without inquiring beyond our pain, our struggles, and the repetitions that keep us eddied in the waters of our life, we can fail to own that our fate is ours—and ours to shift. If we don't do so, we keep small in life.

Your obligation—or your task should you choose to accept it—is to live the life that's yours, not someone else's. The first step to living your life and yours alone is a deeper inquiry into yourself. Cleaning out your closets, if you will. Only then will you be able to undertake the most sacred of all obligations that help us become more human: making the unconscious forces that have been directing your life conscious, confronting that which you've perceived as fate, and transforming it into destiny.

Where Might You Need More Alignment?

If you've ever sat on the question of where to take your business, to scale or to exit, and what impact that might have on your life, thinking about the end of your life can help suss out what's most meaningful and important to you.

For some of us, we have defining moments: lab results, a call from the doctor, or another moment that acts as a threshold: after experiencing it, we can't go back or un-hear what we've heard. The news changes our future, our plans, life, and everything in it.

For some of us, we're lucky to get a coconut of wakefulness lobbed at us, jostling us out of our ill-aligned lives. These moments can make us more alive or give us the courage to step more fully into our lives. We approach them with fortitude, with clarity, and with a hungry sense to suck the marrow out of our life while it's still with us. It's wild, precious, fleeting—and ours.

Now try to imagine the view of your life from your deathbed:

> What have you accomplished?
> What have you left behind?
> How will people remember you?

If you imagine looking back on your life as it is now:

> What stands out?
> What haunts you?
> What is present in that vision, but not present in your life now?
> What would you change in your life now in light of this?

WHERE YOUR LOYALTIES LIE

*Development involves giving up a smaller story
in order to wake up to a larger story.*

—Jean Houston

"You're at midlife," my therapist remarked shortly after my thirty-sixth birthday. I was a little shocked. I was certain I had at least five to ten more years before *midlife* was a fitting term for me.

What feels most like midlife, though, is a big transition point of letting go of a lot of old stories that got me to here, and waking up to a larger story that's much more expansive of the future that's calling me into it. The future that's not encumbered by limits, ties, or bounds to the past. I'm being asked to make room for more of me, my purpose, my work in the world, in ways that I've been held back from fully allowing.

"I've arrived at this place," I said to myself. "What's next? What part of this dream that's flowing through me needs to come forth? How do I make room for that? What do I want to bring with me? What do I want to leave behind?"

And then another question floated in the ether: "What's stopping me?"

I've been wondering what I've been loyal to that isn't serving me and isn't worth carrying forward. Those loyalties and beliefs can be sneaky, becoming a kind of trellis that you grow up around, shaping you more than you shape it. Some part of it feels comfortable, until it doesn't anymore. These trellises contain you, making you feel much smaller than who you are or were meant to be. They make it hard to change and pull towards the direction of that larger story of you.

One of the concepts for these parts of ourselves that keep us small and contained is the notion of the loyal soldier. While loyal soldiers can appear anywhere, I've found they show up around the things I love the most. I met my loyal soldier one summer while looking at a horse, one of my deepest loves that I'd somewhat shoved away for belittling reasons that almost compromised my biggest dream. Once this big four-legged birthday present came into my life, so did a whole slew of voices saying, "You can't do this. It's too expensive. You don't deserve it," and other variations on a core theme of *Whoa! Slow down, pardner. This much happiness and aliveness is not safe.*

Thinking of these sub-personalities of ourselves as loyal soldiers was a concept first developed by Molly Young Brown and described in her book *The Unfolding Self: The Practice of Psychosynthesis*. She had read about a WWII Japanese soldier discovered on a remote island long after the war had ended. When he was rescued, he was shocked to learn that the war was over, and it was difficult for him to give up his fight until he was honored in a parade for his service. This is exactly what happens to parts of ourselves that are intended to keep our lovability, safety, and belonging intact.

As Brown notes, "Our loyal soldiers serve a useful function, keeping us alert and clear about our basic needs and our responsibility to meet them. But they can also limit our creative work in the world if we become identified with their rather myopic perspective. We always have a choice to move beyond this perspective."

How do we begin to see these unseen forces at work in our life? Insert some radical self-inquiry here to avoid being deceived by the reactions coming from your loyal soldiers, and receive—and welcome—them home with compassionate recognition. This is just one way to access your aliveness in its fullness. Otherwise, you live contained and shrunk by these well-meaning and outdated parts of yourself whose pull prevents you from flourishing.

Once you dive in, you'll begin tracking—and then meeting—your loyal soldiers. You will become aware of who or what they sound like, how they feel in your body, and what circumstances tend to call them forth en masse.

To track down where your loyal soldiers show up, consider these questions:

> What is your relationship to risk?

> Where do you choose acceptance by others over your own authenticity?

> How often do you operate to avoid other people's emotions or your fear of their emotional reactions?

> Where do you avoid conflict?

> How do you feel about upsetting or disappointing people?

> How easy is it for you to know what you want and assert what you want? How often do you *just go with the flow* in groups?

> When it comes to hurt and anger that you feel, how do you express it? How often and with whom?

> What does it feel like to stand in your strengths and lean on or lead with your natural abilities or gifts?

> Where, when, and how often do you express your pure exuberance or desires?

> How harsh is your inner critic? When does that inner critic show up? How does it make you feel?

> Where do codependent behaviors such as caretaking, rescuing, and enabling show up in your life? How does a fear of abandonment compel these behaviors?

Our loyal soldiers served to protect us growing up. But in the second half of life, when left unchecked, their soldiers' strategies can dampen our leadership capacities and derail our companies, our relationships, and the full aliveness of who we really are. Their defenses are no longer useful. The primitive coping mechanisms they provided us when we were young no longer fit into our much more complex adult lives. Yet it can take time to disarm them. And it can take more time to hear a much truer voice—that one that sounds like your own.

How can you retire your loyal soldiers, take them out of active duty so you can grow and change? First, identify them. Acknowledge what they did for you, what they were protecting, and why. Thank them for their service. Let them know you survived up till now and you've got this. Your loyal soldiers may need constant reminding before they lay down their arms, and they may come back to make an appearance during times of stress or doubt when they think you need them. If they insist on hanging on for the ride, assure them that they can stay in the backseat, but that your wise adult self has the wheel now.

This whole shift may feel like the longest journey in the world—the distance between your head and your heart. In the process, you're waking those parts of you up to a larger story, ever unfolding. This story includes all that you are and what you're destined to become.

EXILE NOTHING

*The "night sea journey" is the journey into the parts of ourselves
that are split off, disavowed, unknown, unwanted, cast out,
and exiled to the various subterranean worlds of consciousness…
The goal of the journey is to reunite us with ourselves. Such
a homecoming can be surprisingly painful, even brutal. In
order to undertake it, we must first agree to exile nothing.*

—Stephen Cope

Anger is one of those qualities I buried deep in the basement of
my psyche, along with some other gems. My sister and I grew up
watching my father's displays of anger. While he was never physi-
cally violent, when his anger erupted we would calmly watch him
spout off about something, wonder what all the fuss was about,
and look at each other thinking, "WTF is his deal?" I remember
deciding then that I never wanted to be angry, ranting, or out of
control like that.

As I got older I worked to cultivate love and sweetness and light.
I didn't identify with qualities that didn't fit with that self-image.
I was all nonviolent and Gandhi-fied. I was convinced I had those
nasty parts under control. The way I put it was, "In with the good;
out with the bad." But in all that I was setting out to cultivate
within myself, I paved over some key facets of being human—in
fact, I think they had been buried and cut off for a long time—including my connection to my own anger.

Was I angry, even in my undying optimism? Oh, hell yes! That anger was deep in my cells, born perhaps with the original wound of no one being able to ease my suffering as a colicky baby. Later, I'd be mad at decisions my future employers would make. Mad at that the guy who ghosted me after we went out for a month. Mad at vendors that didn't come through and made more work for me. Mad at dealing with people who didn't have their sh*t together.

I was downright pissed off. Many times, righteously so. But did I show it? Barely. Somehow, I managed to keep whatever anger I felt under wraps. I rationalized it from every angle to push that feeling down into "no big deal." When I ranted, it was powerless and full of complaints, laced with more sarcasm than volatility. Or when there was a lot of feeling, my rage would collapse into sadness or grief (read: lots and lots of tears) because tears were somehow more comfortable and acceptable than an expression of anger.

After an awful run-in with my homeowners association—one that left me pissed and shocked but relatively level-headed—my significant other said to me, "But, where's your anger? Aren't you mad?" I looked at him in confusion. It was like that part of my wiring had been unplugged. I didn't feel any charge in the anger department.

In keeping that part of me together for so long, I also dulled other parts of my expression: my spontaneity, my exuberance, my longings. After all, like anger, those traits were also disorderly and unpredictable.

My intensity—all of it, both welcome and unwelcome—was buried along with my anger. By not accessing my denied parts, I failed to experience the potency of my own vitality, and denied my wholeness. We're not all love and light. We've got all the other parts at play in our psyche too. And this is a good thing.

The parts of me that are in my shadow can be brought into the light. At one point, to be safe and fit into my family unit, those shadow parts needed to be held back. But now I don't need to win acceptance from friends and family in order to feel like I fit in my life.

Feeling my anger provides me with useful information. It tells me I have a need that isn't being met or that a boundary has perhaps been crossed. Being angry is not the same as acting angry. Feeling the feeling allows an electricity to flow through me. It powers my ability to stand up for myself.

The things I shoved in the deep, dark place festered. What I thought was quarantined eventually peeked out—and ate at me from the inside—upsetting my highly cultivated norm. It showed up in a larger display of what I don't like in others. Even Rumi notes, "Everybody's scandalous flaw is mine."

I may not have liked my father's outbursts of anger, but I have all of that in me even if I wasn't okay with those parts of me. Over time I've come to find that my relationship to the parts that I don't like in the world are within me too. I often use my reactions such as strong repulsions or tremendous adoration as a clue to my unowned shadow.

To befriend the shadow is to confront the things that appear to assault the image of yourself that you uphold. Instead of fighting off those offending/affronting things, look closely at them and find the recognizable pieces of yourself in each. This is how you welcome in all the parts buried in the deep, stuffed in the basement, or tossed into the black bag behind you.

The trick to shadow reclamation is to exile nothing—each item we discover in our shadow adds to our wholeness. The gift is in reclaiming valuable parts of ourselves that we are now able to employ wisely as adults. Befriending the shadow starts by getting curious about some of your staunch positions and principles, judgements and projections. Look too at virtues you admire in others. These are keys to your disowned positive and negative shadow aspects.

It takes courage, curiosity, and honesty to look for all the ways in which we contradict ourselves. Imagine what befriending all the polarities of ourselves, the dark and the light, can do for our experience of life and our relationships. By embracing all parts of ourselves, we include them in our range of experience. We can begin to know more of our inner terrain and bring it back into the light of consciousness.

Shadow work isn't easy, yet it is essential to becoming better humans. (And we know that better humans make better leaders. And those better leaders create more humane work environments.)

Shadow Tracking: How, Where, and When Does Shadow Show Up?

Grab a pen and paper and jot down responses to these questions:

> How do you handle failure?

> How do you handle conflict? How did your family handle conflict?

> How do you handle chaos and uncertainty?

> What is your greatest fear?

> What was not talked about when you were growing up?

> What behavior do you judge yourself the most for?

> When you think about the people you admire the most, what traits do they have that make you admire them? How can you begin to see these traits in yourself?

> What are the challenges you are facing at work, with colleagues, and/or at home?

> What trait or traits are you most critical of in your teammates, partner, friends, family, or community? Where do you see this trait in yourself?

> What role do you tend to play in relationships?

> When you are defensive, shut down, or reactive when engaging with people, what are you believing about yourself and the world?

What did you learn about yourself in that short exploration? What might you want to explore further with a coach or therapist as a guide?

THE POPULAR VOTE

One does not become enlightened by imagining figures of light, but by making the darkness conscious. The latter procedure, however, is disagreeable and therefore not popular.

—Carl Jung

Like many people, I was shaken to my core by the election results on November 8, 2016. I was reminded of the Reboot podcast episode 51, "The Love That Heals: Welcoming in Our Shadow," in which James Hollis said, "What's wrong in the world is wrong in me as well." As painful as it was, current events proved to be a rich opportunity to look a bit closer at (I cringe as I say this) my inner Trump.

Gah! I didn't think there could be anything more repulsive. But then again, things we have a strong negative or positive reaction to often are cues that a shadow is lurking close. Well, shadow… it's always close.

My first response to the election results was to be viscerally sickened. Hurt. Shock. Horror. Even as I felt a whole range of emotions moving through me, I also felt a deeper response that moved beyond anger to wanting to do something about it. The images conjured up from that place were dark and phantasmagoric about how I could set straight those whose views were vehemently not in line with mine—and set them straight in ways that were particularly violent.

Then I stopped.

There it is. There's my own capacity for the same kind of absurd and real violence I wanted to stand up against.

I rallied to stand up against it all by looking at my own dark spots. Exploring deeper my own dark alleys, I continued to look at all that I loathed about this one figure in the election, then turned all my thoughts around until I could locate a similar vein in me too. Am I capable of manipulation, of saying incredibly hurtful things? How do I keep out and ignore all the views that do not coincide with mine? What are my own tendencies for bullying and narcissism?

How close do I carry uncontested divisiveness between self and other inside me? This wasn't an easy extrapolation. I would have much rather participated in a generative creative imagination, avoiding this altogether by musing about things I love. But something about going to those dark spots was essentially potent, especially the day after the election when I felt eviscerated. The process helped me see that I have those capacities too. It softened my stance and grounded my view in the immediate importance of the explorations of my own inner landscape as the place to start to make change—for my life, my relationships, my community, and my world.

In *Why Good People Do Bad Things: Understanding Our Darker Selves*, James Hollis writes:

> It takes a strong sense of self, and no little courage, to be able to examine, and take responsibility for, these darker selves when they turn up. It is much easier to deny, blame others, project elsewhere, or bury it and just keep on rolling. It is at these moments of human frailty when we are most dangerous to ourselves, our families, and our society. Examining this material is not a form of self-indulgence; it is a way of taking responsibility for our choices and their consequences. It is

an act of great moral moment, for it brings the possibility of lifting our stuff off of others, surely the most ethical and useful thing we can do for those around us.

Not only do we lift our stuff off others, we also make conscious and recognize the very real and present shadowed aspects of our own personality. And when we glimpse our shadow qualities, what do we do then? By pulling these things out of shadow, we are welcoming back parts of ourselves that we've kept hidden or divided ourselves from. Accepting these are part of who we are is a radical act of conscious recovery of our wholeness. It's a way of loving ourselves all the way down and all the way through, dark spots and all.

When we "think globally, act locally" in our inner landscape—that most immediate landscape that affects everything in our life—we free our partners, children, organizations, and communities from the burden of living through and acting out our unresolved issues. That, my friends, is the gift of nonviolence. Of peace. Of freedom.

While looking at the shadow closest to home may not be your ego's first pick, it will surely be the popular vote of your soul. Solely casting that vote proves to be a healing balm for many. Perhaps it is imperative for those of us having a human experience on this planet to do this work to heal the collective psyche.

In his book *The Eden Project: In Search of the Magical Other*, Hollis writes:

> For the individual to heal, he or she must recover a better relationship to soul. For corporate bodies to heal, they must have managers who will address the question of soul. And we cannot expect them to do this for their companies if they have not done it for themselves. As Jung repeatedly warned, the therapist cannot accompany the patient any further than the therapist has gone. Therefore, the willingness to

address one's personal healing is essential before one can contribute a measure of healing to the collective.

I reached out to my therapist post-election to share my feelings. "Periodically, the world falls apart," he said, "and it is held together by the good, patient, steady work of people like you until the world heals again, for a while."

FINDING YOU IN THE THICK OF IT

When the intersection of life and work isn't proving successful by some measure we feel it should be, we are often quick to wonder if this isn't what we're supposed to be doing. Any moment like that can make us wobble in our own grounding sense of where we are and what we know right here. I've been there with my art. I've been there with other jobs. It can feel so crushing. Without ground, it can feel like we're without a compass, unable to trust our read of the situation. It shakes up the faith we have in ourselves, among other things.

One of the books I returned to often as a little human was the story of Louis Pasteur, called *The Value of Believing in Yourself.* Its worn pages retell the story of the scientist whose unwavering belief in the concept of germs eventually led to a cure for rabies. Despite disbelief from others, hurdles, and the lack of enthusiasm he encountered along the way, Pasteur believed in what he knew and marched on, following his gut and his research.

When I think of him soldiering on, sworn to his convictions, I wonder what lessons in self-faith he could offer us in the moments we feel stuck in the corners of our passions. When we feel it's right but also find ourselves wondering why it feels so hard: "Why am I not getting traction? Why is no one buying the product? Why am I not making any money?"

I like to think that much of what we encounter in our lives, and perhaps most especially in our work lives, offers itself up to our healing in some way if we choose to work with it as such. When work life feels messy, or it's not going how we intended, it's hard to think that anything beneficial could be happening. Yet I've learned to trust that those sticky situations, like the ones that you'd rather cherry-pick through, usually have a worthwhile kernel of experience and wisdom readily available.

When things feel unruly, when we feel undone, frayed, and frazzled, it's a practice to see that there might be something emerging through all the chaos. If we can sit and stay in the thick of it, and make a habit of inquiring within from that place, we can work with what's arising and what parts of us may be growing.

Personal growth and healing aren't tidy. Sometimes our process gets messier before it gets better and the good stuff shakes out. Each scenario of what looks like "deep, messy human healing in progress" bears a constellation of conscious and subconscious choices and motivations. And when I've been in those places, there are a few things that helped me reframe where I'm at so I can see things in a different light, and see myself differently within it.

When I have the wherewithal to inquire into myself in those moments (enter radical self-inquiry), I hope to catch a glimpse of the psychological threads that hold me there. Feeling stuck, one part of me wants to move ahead and another part feels magnetized to repeat old patterns. Here I wonder, "What does this situation hold for me that I need to unravel and heal before I can move past it more harmoniously?"

Life will tend to dish up lessons until they are learned, or until a new perspective is realized. When the path starts to feel familiar, the dynamics at play can bear a striking resemblance to the past: Why do I always find myself in these situations? That's when we can begin to realize that some conscious or, most likely, subconscious part of us keeps choosing this scenario. Who is that part of us? What does that part of us want for us? What's important to them? What do they need?

As entrepreneurs, we have ample opportunity to inquire deeply into what's coming up for us in the moments we face. If we can withstand those times that make us ask "Is this what I'm supposed to be doing?" we will find ourselves in a growth moment. If we can return to our wise selves, we can ride the waves without losing faith in ourselves in the process. From there, the answers to those ungrounding wonderings can come to us as we find our way through the adventures we didn't expect.

Part II

UNFOLDING YOUR AUTHENTIC SELF

EMOTIONS AS DATA POINTS

Emotional congruence builds trust. Feelings come before thoughts. Yet sometimes we can feel so much and not know what to do with it all. Every wave of emotional energy—from sadness to joy, anger to fear—brings with it information if we pay attention. This is integral to leading and living an examined life. It's also akin to being authentic and living in integrity. To do so, and do it well enough, we must create the space to sort through our experience.

How can we sort through the emotional weather patterns we experience throughout our days and mine the data from those moments and plot twists? When we build our emotional competence, we build inner congruence, which helps us say what we need to say. It helps us understand our fears and what we want and need. We may find, then, that next steps and decisions come with more ease.

For example, I might notice that I'm having judgmental thoughts. Those thoughts aren't bad and having them isn't wrong. However, if I berate myself for being judgmental or believing those thoughts, then I could head down a path I may not ultimately want to traverse. What I can do is notice those thoughts and notice that I'm having the experience of being judgmental. What, then, does that information tell me? What brought those thoughts to the surface? What might I be feeling underneath that? How might those thoughts be pointing to an implicit agenda I have or a belief I have? How might that information help me understand myself better, or help me identify a fear, need, or wish?

Tuning in to our emotional data is part of tuning in to our inner compass. Doing so creates the space needed to check in and parse our emotional data points. With those fresh insights, we can choose a response that directs our progress forward with more alignment, resolve, and maybe even sanity.

This being an entrepreneur is a guesthouse; every morning a new arrival. Even when you do it all right, less desirable things can happen.

Withstanding this roller coaster of an experience is what good entrepreneurs do. It's what they sign up for. They have taken the risk and the freedom of doing their own thing their way. At the intersection of freedom and risk is their lived experience—sometimes turbulent, sometimes terrifying, sometimes lit up (in a good way). The range of emotions for the varied experiences that show up on any given day can be a wild ride, but it's what the soulful entrepreneur shows up for.

See, the soulful entrepreneur doesn't leave their experience: they are in it. They've traded the risks of full-catastrophe living and working for their freedom and autonomy. They face things head-on and get on by going through whatever it is that's coming their way—be it cash flow, communication issues, press coverage, or COVID. There's no transcending here.

A spoonful of chicken soup for the entrepreneur's soul might be this: This is hard. You are alive doing this thing that calls for living intensely—the burn of embarrassment, the anxiety of losing control as the company grows, the dread of looking at the P&L of the down months, the pit in your belly, the racing heart from that email bomb, the thrill of the sale, and the places in our body that carry our tension, worry, fears, excitement, and elations. Soul includes the whole of your life—the messy along with the tidy. Living these moments is embodying the soul of the entrepreneur.

SINCE FEELING IS FIRST

My most favorite lines of poetry are from E. E. Cummings:

> since feeling is first
> who pays any attention
> to the syntax of things
> will never wholly kiss you

I love juxtaposing these lines from Cummings's poem "Since Feeling is First" to our startup cultures in which engineering is highly valued or where life is trying to be hacked into a calculus. Humans are more complex than that. As an amazing human yourself, you know this: you can't engineer a kiss.

All of life is to be felt. It's coursing through us all the time. Sometimes we feel so much yet don't know what to do with it all.

Fear is a potent one. Its various fight-flight-or-freeze tendencies can wash over us in ways that are ultimately uncomfortable, as if our very lives are at stake. It's a feeling we all know. Sometimes these fears arrive quietly, without any real threat, perhaps with just a thought. Whichever way they assume their takeover, I've learned that if I don't voice my fears they will control me in ways that are less than positive.

One of the tools that has helped me get more intimate with all the feels I might be feeling—especially fear—is a practice of listening to my body. This can be as simple as asking, What are these feelings trying to tell me? Or, the more in-depth practice rolls like this...

> What body sensations do you notice? Where do you feel them? What do you feel in that location?

> What core emotions do you notice?

> Fill in any details that come with the sensation, such as:

- I see the image of _____.
- Words that came to me were _____.
- I hear a voice saying _____.

> What does this remind you of from the past?

Then breathe. Take a moment to appreciate what you're experiencing.

When I have employed this practice, whatever feeling I may have been avoiding I see in a new light. By getting curious, I change my relationship to it. I can then be present with it and myself, and with that information revealed the next step becomes clearer. Such a practice is a tool to bring into your daily life as a leader, parent, and partner.

THE TURNING

Ever felt a bit like Dante in his infamous *Inferno*? "Midway on our life's journey, I found myself in dark woods, the right road lost." He doesn't remember how he lost his true path but he's wandered into a fearful place, a dark and tangled valley. As he attempts to climb up and out towards the light, a series of characters chase him back down into the wild, impenetrable wood. (It's worth noting that Dante is about thirty-five years old at this juncture. You know, midlife.)

Maybe you can relate.

Acute existential depression—versus chronic or clinical depression—surfaces at various points in our lives as an angst, which isn't a *bad* thing to be cured. Our feelings are to be felt, not solved. Feelings, even our loudest ones, have a lot of information. In a sense, they are messengers. This is especially true in periods of existential depression. When this form of depression finds us, we must ask ourselves, "What is the message here for me now?"*

So often our emotional literacy is tested when we find ourselves in the dark and twisted woods, having lost our true path. Perhaps what worked for us in the past isn't working for us now. Or we know what might work, but we can't muster up the gumption to try. It's a tough spot to be in and one that we'd often rather medicate,

---

* I want to be very clear that I'm not talking about clinical depression, which is a serious mental health issue that requires the help of psychological or medical professionals.

gloss over, bypass, or somehow erase due to the intensity of some less than good feelings. We fight it, failing to accept the dark cloud hanging over us, and failing to seek whatever silver lining may exist.

Parker Palmer, who shares his struggles with depression in his book *Let Your Life Speak*, tells us what his friend said to him when one of the dark seasons was moving in on his life: "You seem to look upon depression as the hand of an enemy trying to crush you. Do you think you could see it instead as the hand of a friend, pressing you down to the ground on which it is safe to stand?"

What if our existential depression is asking us to listen more closely to the nudges and whispers that we may have squashed or silenced in lieu of another, more assertive and reasonable voice? What if this dark and tangled wood is the place from which we reconnect with our true path? What if the message for us in the dark seasons is showing us what's not working and what needs to change?

"The most fundamental aggression to ourselves, the most fundamental harm we can do to ourselves," Pema Chödrön writes in *When Things Fall Apart: Heart Advice for Difficult Times*, "is to remain ignorant by not having the courage and the respect to look at ourselves honestly and gently."

When we look at ourselves honestly and gently, we can begin to see where we're off track, where parts of us are not aligned—not only with others but primarily with ourselves. Sometimes, much like Dante's adventure through the Inferno, this can feel like hell because we may have to look at some hard stuff in our life and psyche. To right ourselves—to turn—means bringing our parts into alignment, to include the parts we've repressed and welcome back parts we've abandoned. This includes our truest gifts and our essence, as well as the intense-feelings parts of our story that we've tried to slice off along the way.

"The opposite of play isn't work," asserts Stuart Brown, the founder of the National Institute for Play. "It's depression."

Consider these questions as you check in on how closely all parts of *you* are in alignment:

> What drags you down and drains your energy?
> What part of you keeps you from the thing you most want, and the thing that makes you feel most alive?
> What part of you has lost a sincere, unswerving commitment to your life?
> When did you stop laughing?
> How do you keep out the sweet territory of silence?

The turning begins when we true up our inner and outer selves to live divided no more. Here, we become who we are meant to become, step-by-step, on our true path. This happens when we connect more deeply to ourselves and the quiet voice within, when we connect to our perceptible body more deeply, and when we allow our whole self to show up completely—no matter what emotional weather pattern may be passing by.

When we lose congruence within ourselves, we lose a connection not just to our inner world and our own presence, but to the lifelines around us: our friends, relatives, colleagues, community, the flora and fauna, the natural world. It's as if the dark wood holds us down in a place that's safe to stand, as wild and terrifying as it may have become, reminding us who we really are and what we're here to do.

Like any great turning in our lives, we don't know what it is until we're past it. It's a thing we find our way through by feeling our way into it. By getting quiet and listening to that still, inner voice, or to the beat-beat-whisper of our heart, and trusting it. Or perhaps as Dante did, we can find a wise guide like Virgil to lead us through the Inferno. While these phases feel like rough patches we'd rather race through, busy ourselves through, or somehow forget, sometimes we need to pause and get grounded. Then we can ask what lessons are in front of us as we face struggles, feelings of helplessness, and existential experiences.

In those moments, how do we remember that who we are is neither what is happening to us nor where we happen to be? There's a still quiet voice that knows us and what we need and want. When we find ourselves lost in the dark woods, a key to our resiliency is to listen, closely, to that voice…and what brings our hearts alive.

"You are the sky," Pema Chödron famously said. "Everything else is just the weather."

SPIRIT MEETS BONE

Almost anybody can learn to think or believe or know, but not a single human being can be taught to feel. Why? Because whenever you think or you believe or you know, you're a lot of other people: but the moment you feel, you're nobody-but-yourself.

To be nobody-but-yourself—in a world which is doing its best, night and day, to make you everybody else—means to fight the hardest battle which any human being can fight; and never stop fighting.

—E. E. Cummings

How you walk through the world shapes your experiences and relationships, as well as what you create. How you walk through the world is informed by the "soft stuff"—the heart wisdom that is often skirted around as we reach for the next playbook to follow. Yet we miss out on a great deal of magic when we opt for someone else's how-to.

To borrow a line from singer-songwriter Lucinda Williams, "down where the spirit meets the bone" is where the moments "you're nobody-but-yourself" take shape. This is where your consciousness manifests in the meatsuit you received at birth. The intricate physiology of your unique meatsuit is the lived-in terrain only you know. From time to time, other authors, poets, and colleagues may put into words the nuances that you perceive, but it's your particular feelers that know the world as only you know it.

Discovering the edges and excavating the terrain of your lived-in map is inherent in the process of becoming an adult. As you venture through life, digging into the heart-mind-body complex that is *you* is a good investment with both immediate and long-term returns. It's a solo gig, however, so consider this your very own perpetual studio space.

There's no playbook for being yourself. Playbooks are entirely limiting as you set out into this work. This is the path to doing the work of your life.

Poet John O'Donohue, in *To Bless the Space Between Us: A Book of Blessings*, reminds us that "each of us is an artist of our days. The greater our integrity and awareness, the more original and creative our time will become."

The intersect where the inner and outer worlds connect is a space we're always navigating as humans, what we move through moment to moment. Each world interconnects like two circles in a Venn diagram. In the middle, the place of overlap, is the sweet spot. There, where the edge of the two worlds meet, is the creative horizon and your ability to dance with it. And to be clear, that sweet spot can be elusive to find and scary to surrender to.

It's not always unicorns and rainbows at the overlap. The seat of the soul is where spirit meets bone, where things get truly real, and where the burning heat of the pulse under our skin is the tide on which feelings and thoughts arise in response to our situation and environment. When big questions loom with a sense of impending doom, navigating those edges feels trickier, harder perhaps, or maybe even terrifying. What's at stake when we shy away from our edges? We lose our connection to that sweet spot.

As Seth Godin notes in the "How to Walk through the World" episode of the Reboot podcast, "It's important to distinguish between the feeling in your heart and the feeling in your amygdala.*

---

* The amygdala is a small, almond-sized structure in the brain. It is a major processing center for emotions, especially fear, in both humans and animals. It also has a big role in memory, learning, habits, and social understanding.

Likewise, there's no getting around our humanity by using the heart stuff to bypass the amygdala. Sorting through all of that, we arrive at the core of who we are behind the façades: the who we think we are and the who we think we want to be. Determining what's what creates space for something else to find us in the moments when we're unregulated, when nothing makes sense, and when we wish there was a pill for our humanity.

When you reach the edge of your map of the known world with the known-knowns and the known-unknowns, what then? Are you fortified to handle the unknown-unknowns? What do you do when you're afraid? How do you get your butterflies in order? (See essay "Red Light Moments" on page 75 for more about getting your butterflies in order.) And what's on the other side of that? What happens when you can walk calmly into the places that could scare you?

At Reboot's first bootcamp in Tuscany years ago, I was sitting poolside with a bootcamper who turned to me and said, "I started this company fully intending to do something different, to lead differently, and create a company worth working for. But I find myself stuck and feeling worse. I don't know if I should quit."

"Sometimes, when you ask for what you want, you get all of the lessons you need to get to where you want to end up," I replied. "Maybe you're right where you need to be."

Traversing the way from where you are to where you want to be isn't always as easy as we envision. Getting to what we'd like involves passing through the parts of us that hold us back or don't think it's such a great idea in the first place. Discovering how our psyche works and becoming well-versed in peering at what's in the shadows of our inner landscape helps us uncover what stops us, where our inner critic lives and what provokes it, and what big emotional burdens we've been carrying that keep us from moving forward and aren't ours to carry.

What happens in the studio of *you* is of utmost importance. As we set out to do work that we're proud of, or live a life according to our own definition of success, there are those unknown-unknowns we face. In that quiet and teeming place where spirit meets bone, we can find our way through at the edges of we-don't-know-what-quite-yet.

The edge of you coming together with the edge of something else has the potential to create a third, much greater thing. It's a new way of being with and in the world. That process of discovery is an oft-overlooked high art where, over years, mastery happens. It's where good work happens. It's where you do the work of your life. So ask yourself:

> What's moving you and moving through you?

> What's informing you in new ways?

> How can you draw on this when life throws you unseen challenges and boons in brilliant disguises?

> When do you feel most like yourself?

THE STRESS OF WORK LIFE

Back in the day, I was lured by the buzz around the startup scene and set out to leave my role at a scrappy local web development and full-stack online marketing company to join the excitement and thrill and fun work that was waiting for me there. "I want to work with the cool kids," I said to myself. And, sure enough, I did. The day before my birthday that year, I handed in my resignation and signed up for my new role running Ops for the hippest little dev shop in town.

Do you ever think you really, really want one thing, and then when you get it you wonder frantically to yourself, WTF was I thinking?

After one month I found myself right in the middle of startup life, that charming chaos which at first feels like being in a relationship with someone with borderline personality disorder. I was so stressed that I would go home at night, lie on my floor and cry, and wonder what was wrong with me—as if I was doing something wrong. I mean, we had the coolest office downtown, a fridge stocked with organics, a team of rad people, great clients, an indoor garden! Wasn't this supposed to be work heaven? Why did I feel so awful?

In my case, I powered on, determined to get through each day. In the midst of trying to make sense of my feelings and figuring out how to keep my soul intact even though it felt like it was being sucked out of me, my body started saying *No* in various and obvious ways. I'll spare you the details but, in short, that experience opened the door to a tough bout with chronic illness which had upended many of my body's systems from working properly.

Stress wreaks havoc on the body in more ways than many of us type-A worker bees care to admit. The body will let you know in subtle and not-so-subtle ways when it says no, in the hope that you'll listen. Yet so often we don't catch our body's memo—or blow past it—until we can't ignore it anymore. Add to that the internalized stressors of a dysfunctional and toxic work environment, and you've got the perfect storm for stress to erode health and for illness to take hold.

What keeps us going headlong, hunkering down towards what we think we want, come hell or high water, even though our experience is taxing us greatly? What keeps us driven to adrenal fatigue? What keeps us moving at mach-five-with-our-hair-on-fire, compulsively driven towards an ideal, a vision, cloaked in a delusional sense of purpose while our body revolts against that whole notion? What other signs and knowings are we blowing past or brushing aside? What is whispering to us to stop? Why might we be afraid to listen?

It's not just the stress of the do-more-faster mentality, the pressures of VC funding or lack thereof, or the turbulent iterations and pivoting of startup life that can slay us slowly. In the entrepreneurial context, our mental game and our unowned shadow qualities set our resilience capacity to handle all that's moving towards us and all that we're moving through. How we feel about work, the thoughts we keep running, and what triggers us can compound our experience of stress just as much as environmental factors. Here at Reboot, we see this all the time in entrepreneurs who are burned out.

Our bodies are wired to respond to stress with our fight-or-flight response. Then the surge of blood and chemicals stops, and the body returns to normal, relieved to have survived. What happens for us humans in the face of the unrelenting stressors of, say, life and work is that our body never has a break in the action of the mental and emotional stressors that bear down on us. Genuine emotional stress, such as when a loved one dies or an awful breakup happens, can shake up the nervous system in a similar way. The body holds on to that as if the tiger is at your heels, and it's fighting to survive—continuously.

Emotional stress is just as real as environmental stress and loss of control, lack of information, and uncertainty. Anything that threatens our sense of safety, belonging, and being loved causes turmoil for our nervous system.

This is why early imprinting in childhood can have such a stronghold on both our sense of self and our wellness and resilience by setting up the structures that wire our responses to the world. When love, safety, or belonging is threatened for a newborn human, the primal part of our brain wants to survive. It will do whatever it takes not to die—the most important self-preservation programming. In fact, most trade-offs we make to avoid death at an early age are to trade what we have, which is almost nothing. So we give away our own well-being, such as our right to need (ask for things) or our right to exist (be seen or stand up for what we believe). Those early rote neurological patterns run over and over again to ensure our continued survival, yet they can form outdated beliefs that lead to ways of being in the world and become the brain's default path.

As humans, we all have early patterning that is affecting us now, unconsciously. Those old programs may not be serving us in our work environments if they are affecting our reactions to situations we encounter. Hans Selye, renowned Canadian researcher on stress and author of *The Stress of Life*, notes, "It's not stress that kills us, it's our reaction to it."

When it comes to peeking under the hood to see what's driving you, it helps to look at your shadow qualities for clues. This requires radical self-inquiry, including exploration of emotional spaces that scare you—like things you've shoved in that dark, deep-down place—to see what you're really up to. Only then can you begin to untangle the neural pathways that formed in the earliest history of you. Without inquiring deeper to explore parts of yourself, you may find that you're spinning your wheels, unaware and unable to change—or falling into chronic illness—and failing to see that there are other choices besides the ones that may have become rote.

Ready to begin exploring what's under the hood of you? Consider the following:

> What feels stressful?

> Where do you feel stuck?

> If there was an image or picture of what you feel about your stress or stuckness, what does it look like?

> Where is your aliveness stifled?

> What patterns or behaviors are creating stress (e.g., people pleasing, perfectionism)?

> What in your environment is creating stress (e.g., unclear expectations, uncertainty, bullying)?

> What would you like to experience instead of the above?

> Who could you reach out to for support?

When you know what you'd like to be experiencing and what keeps you stuck, you are less likely to be driven by delusion and more likely to be lovingly devoted to what you want—by your own conscious choosing.

RED LIGHT MOMENTS

How many times do we lose an occasion for soul work by leaping ahead to final solutions without pausing to savor the undertones? We are a radically bottom-line society, eager to act and to end tension, and thus we lose opportunities to know ourselves for our motives and our secrets.

—Thomas Moore, *Care of the Soul: A Guide for Cultivating Depth and Sacredness in Everyday Life*

Our responses to trigger events can come on so fast it may seem as if we are hardwired that way. Regardless of where we learned our style, or what events provoke responses as if a switch has been flipped that puts us "in the red," learning to find the pause button between stimulus and response grants us time to sort out what's really going on when our amygdala is hijacked. That awareness cultivates a muscle that can spark our curiosity to learn more and choose how we want to respond.

While creating that pause for ourselves (and our relationships) is important, doing so when your switches have been flipped isn't always easy. Hair-trigger responses can take time to undo, as do long-standing and hard-learned ways of reacting to the world. Learning to find our pause button can be a game-changer for ourselves, our relationships, and our companies.

In her book *Animals in Translation: Using the Mysteries of Autism to Decode Animal Behavior*, Temple Grandin notes that the only difference that's obvious to the naked eye between human and animal brains is the increased size of the neocortex in humans. (The neocortex includes the frontal lobes as well as all the other structures where higher cognitive functions, like reason and language, are located.) The lower-level structures of the brain—such as the amygdala, which is the seat of emotions in both people and animals, as mentioned earlier—look identical. She writes:

> To understand why animals seem so different from normal human beings, yet so familiar at the same time, you need to know that the human brain is really three different brains, each one built on top of the previous at three different times in evolutionary history. And here's the really interesting part: each one of those brains has its own kind of intelligence, its own sense of time and space, its own memory, and its own subjectivity. It's almost as if we have three identities inside our heads, not just one.

When I'm working with my horse, I often feel that I'm working with the parts of the human brain we sometimes forget about, such as those parts that evolved well before the prefrontal cortex. We may pretend we have evolved past this primitive neurology, but that's just our wordy-language and abstractly rational side making up stories.

For the equine nervous system, new experiences with unknown things can be perceived as a death sentence and, therefore, very scary. Sometimes this instinct kicks in with something seemingly benign to us two-leggeds, like a plastic bag or newspapers blowing in the wind. The horse that can venture into the unknown and manage his own reaction of fear to whatever scary things lie ahead can lead the rest of the herd through whatever it is that's terrifying (if they haven't run away already).

While working on loading my horse into the horse trailer this fall, I was guided by a local horsewoman who referred to the ability for the horse to manage his reactions as "getting his butterflies in order." The horse that can manage his butterflies in a herd can lead the rest of the herd through the new situation. For a horse to be able to organize his butterflies, he has to learn to pause versus react when those fight-flight-freeze survival instincts loom large. Once a horse can learn to master a pause that allows him to shift from fear to curiosity about how to move forward (or not), he can turn to his human for support, and thus become a good partner with his human (versus being so lost in fear that he forgets he's got a human partner with him, which can lead to dangerous scenarios—something you want to avoid when working with a 1,200-pound animal with a well-evolved survival response).

The equine brain, with its much smaller prefrontal cortex, operates only slightly differently than ours. As human mammals, we have our own lived versions of reactions to plastic bags. We can also learn to help ourselves get our butterflies in order when we have a strong emotional reaction to something blowing in (or seemingly blowing in) our path, thanks to a bit more gray matter where it matters.

When it comes to learning how to insert a pause between our highly emotional responses, we have to learn to exercise the pathway to our higher brain functions, which can add seconds to process the trigger as we mull over the events that just happened. Otherwise, the stimulus comes in and the amygdala generates our response in lightning-fast time. By lessening our reactivity and giving us time to choose a wise action, the ability to take a pause can not only abort an amygdala hijack moment but avoid one altogether.

To be clear, tending to our butterflies as humans doesn't involve suppressing our feelings. It involves mastering our own ability to pause between stimulus and response. When something happens (stimulus) we're charged to react (in a way we may or may not be proud of). If we stop to check in with ourselves about what is happening and how we'd like to move forward or not, we create space where we can stop to wonder, with no pressure to go anywhere or do anything. When we mind this gap, we build our own resilience with whatever metaphorical newspapers and plastic bags we encounter.

As humans, the only things we can control are our choices and actions. The ability to respond with aplomb versus a bomb of a reaction can create openings instead of closings, space for curiosity as opposed to rigid stances. It gives us a chance to pause and wonder about what's going on for us before reacting hot and fast.

A red light moment gives us a chance to evaluate, even just a little:

> What just happened?
> What am I feeling?
> What does this remind me of?
> What is important to me right now?
> What do I need?
> What am I willing to ask for?

Widening this gap between stimulus and response is a practice that gets easier with use. Taking care and taking charge of our butterflies gives us a chance to check in with ourselves and how we're doing. This is a form of tending to, one of self-care and discovery. By leaning into those spaces in ourselves, we open up the opportunity to meet others and life from a more generative and generous place. We find our growth and freedom when we can heed that space.

AN INSIDE JOB

Ever felt not enough? Not good enough? Not smart enough? Not liked enough? It could even sound like this:

I don't work out enough.
I'm not productive enough.
I'm not happy enough.

Such feelings are bound to show up at work, while scrolling social media, or in any scenario that equates our sense of self-worth with our output. When the results don't match up (and they rarely do), we doubt our inherent lovability. We spiral into some semblance of anxiety—maybe even shame, and certainly self-loathing—at our self-perceived inadequacy. All of which makes us feel pretty bad instead of feeling pretty bad-ass.

This pervasive feeling can be an indicator of imposter syndrome, but also stands alone as its own phenomenon of wallowing in an impaired sense of our own worth. When we're stuck there, we forget that "I am" is a complete sentence, and our boundaries become weak. We fall prey to the corrosive effects of letting the external world bolster the places where we're unsupportive in our own selves.

Often tied to a harsh inner critic, the feeling of *not enough* drives us to unattainable goals of perfection. We can push ourselves hard—to exhaustion, to depression—if we heed the unrelenting inner voices that motivate us in those directions. But if we listen closely to these voices, what do they say? What happens if we don't deliver, produce, work hard, etc.? What are the consequences? What would be enough? Who's doing the measuring here?

When we seek validation of our worth from external forces, we're often searching for love, safety, or belonging—a reassuring sense that we are okay. If we can parse our self-critical mind, we can hone in on unconscious factors that may be driving our behaviors. By listening closely, as if with a glass to the wall of our brain, we may begin to ascertain some voices that sound familiar. Spending some time there may help us untangle its true meaning.

It's the search for reassurance from outside ourselves that can be problematic for those of us aspiring to become mature adults.

As kids, we're not always given the quintessential message that we are okay as we are. Instead, we may have grown up in a world where we internalized that we needed to perform, or do, or be a certain way, in order to be loved, be safe, or belong in the family unit. This shifts the locus of our self-worth meter away from our inner knowing. And as we become adults, those voices can feel less like the call to safety as was intended, and more like a torture chamber of emotional and verbal self-flagellation.

How we talk to ourselves is often not how we would talk to other people, at least in our outside voice. This tone of our inner dialogue can tell us something important, and we must not take this harshness of our inner voice for granted. How we think on the inside is just as crucial as what we speak aloud. When we notice our inner voice veering towards cruelty, it is a sign that we must move towards a kindness to ourselves and question those non-helpful tones in our inner dialogues.

It's safe to say that a case of the *not-good-enoughs* is an inside job, one we must tend to if we want to emerge into adulthood with the freedom that comes from knowing we're loved just as we are. Sometimes that deeply internalized, highly judgmental voice sounds like Mom, Dad, or another prominent caregiver. It's as if these tapes get lodged in our brain's database in a defragmented way, perhaps even with faulty information. What gets stuck in a memory plays out on repeat within us, like a bug in the system. Due to the nature of memory and the deletion, distortion, and generalization that happens, what replays can be more like a misheard lyric. Once we learn where our inner critic came from and what it meant for us, we can modify the amplification and bring it down to appropriate size.

Regardless of how our body logged the information, the constellation of emotions and meaning tied to that imprinted memory can shape our whole life. Our sense of worth can be established by beliefs we create before we can even talk. These get lodged into our wiring in a slightly deeper way, where they become core to our forming identity and something that can play out throughout our life.

Author Sera Beak sums the nature of core wounds in this excerpt from her book *Redvelations: A Soul's Journey to Becoming Human*:

> Psychologists know that core wounds can happen at any time, but tend to occur when we are between zero to two years old, which means we can be wounded while in the womb. We become wounded from many different things, such as not being picked up one time when we are crying in our crib, ongoing neglect, abuse, the absence of a parent, preferential treatment of a sibling during a fight, or overhearing a family member say something unkind about us, and so on.

She continues:

> Because most of us are wounded at such a young age, it's not biologically safe for us to blame our caregivers (yet) because they are our only means of survival and appear like gods to us... So, we blame ourselves instead. We come up with reasons for why this happened to us, which usually results in the belief that it happened because something is (very) wrong with us. We create these false beliefs about ourselves often when we are preverbal.

However, as adults it's important to become conscious of, and try to verbalize, the beliefs that formed in reaction to the wound because they influence our decisions, generate our behaviors, and stimulate our strategies. Most commonly, we try to prove that we are the opposite of our wound-based beliefs, which often propels us to do what we do in our life (or lives). So, for example, if we unconsciously believe we are worthless, we will try to prove that we are valuable and strive to be the best financier, mother, spiritual teacher, surgeon, or coach.

There's a lot going on inside all of us. The road to loving ourselves requires finding and tending to all the things we're not even consciously aware of that are keeping us from resourcing the love we seek from within our own self (versus from our friends, partners, employers, or anyone we project our wounded caregiver relationships on to).

When the external defines whether or not you are okay, that's a broken system. It keeps you at the whim and whimsy of anything but your own anchor. We live in a world where our value is measured by our output versus who we are. As the beloved Fred Rogers notes in his book *You Are Special: Neighborly Words of Wisdom from Mister Rogers*, "When we love a person, we accept him or her exactly as is: the lovely with the unlovely, the strong with the fearful, the true mixed in with the façade, and of course, the only way we can do it is by accepting ourselves that way."

Learning to love yourself is a broad stroke of self-compassion—the cornerstone to self-care. Living from that place allows us to resource our security from a different place, an internal place, where we know that we're okay. From here, we can give ourselves what we are looking out to the world to give us. And, in that sense, we are healed. Perhaps from here, instead of striving to prove ourselves to the world, we can begin to internalize that it's not our output but our well-being that is our great contribution to life.

Rightsizing Your Inner Critic

Even on the brightest of days, not lurking too far in the shadows are the monsters in our heads. They whisper things that make us second-guess ourselves by cutting us down, weighing in a heavy critique, confirming where we're too much or not enough, and a cacophony of other things no one likes to hear. Though these internal mutterings might sound ludicrous against the backdrop of the reality of our lives and the inherent goodness of who we are, some part of us gets convinced: Maybe they are right.

Some clients call this their "gremlin," or their "mean voice" or the "sh*tty committee." We've all got one: it's the place where the opinionated voices in our head loudly heckle us as we go through our days. While some voices are more feral than others, they often confirm our worst fears about ourselves. If we listen to them, we spiral in an unpleasant emotional domino effect.

When these voices lob their loud critiques at us, it's hard for us to just…be who we are. Our job as humans is to help these voices find their rightful place (and volume) so that we are free and unfettered to be who we are—shamelessly.

What do those monsters need so that they will no longer rob you of your most fully lived life, and most importantly, so that the world can experience the fullness of who you are?

To learn more about your inner critic, here are some questions to help you discover it:

> What does your inner critic sound like? What does it say?

> Who does it sound like?

> When does it show up or get really loud?

> What is important to that inner critic? What does it want most for you?

> How would it dress if it was in human form?

> Does it have a name? If not, give it one.

> What would you like your inner critic to know about you?

THE PERILS OF PERFECTIONISM

Perfection has many faces. I'm sure you've seen it in yourself or in people you know in varying façades. It's characterized by high standards of performance fueled by a fear of failure, accompanied by critical self-evaluations, and often highly concerned about what others think—as if the outside world holds the scorecard for one's accomplishments or appearance or value. We can find perfection close to the bone when it shows up in the images we uphold about ourselves, and our relationship with anything that looks like failure.

In the business world, perhaps we feel our worth is measured by our ROI. For instance, we can see our own thoughts pounce into measuring our self-worth when someone else's company is crowned a unicorn and we're not. What thoughts rattle in our heads then? What conversations do we have with ourselves? My guess is they aren't gentle and compassionate.

I can feel an undercurrent of it in myself whenever I fall into comparison. Heaven knows the internet is perfect for going down that road to nowhere, fast. We see it in the faces online, in the person whose number of likes on their social media highlight reel fuels their sense of self-worth. I see it in highly manicured online presences and often wonder who the *real* person is behind the polished content, the online marketing, and large mailing lists.

Delegating the measure of your worth to external sources is risky business unless you have a penchant for self-loathing.

Sometimes you can almost see or feel the empty ghosts that may run someone's life, veering them to the glossiest new thing, silently hoping to be liked, fit in, win, and get further away from their felt sense of self-loathing. Yet for these empty vortexes, it doesn't matter what glossy things, new gadgets, billions, millions, or brands are craved, desired, or brought into its never satisfied gullet: it's empty because there's nothing to hold it. Nothing external can fill that gaping void.

When we fight with perfectionism, we yield the weapons of delusion towards ourselves. We find a denial of "what is" and instead find piles of delusions about who we are and the stories we tell about ourselves. It's a space that is narrow and incongruent, that fails to include all parts of us, that fails to include our wholeness.

Who are we without the masks that keep us from our authentic selves? What do we tell ourselves? The incongruence of the face you front to the world and who you really are is a rejection of…who you really are. That's an exhausting act to uphold in the up and down, left and right and back again, squiggly spaghetti line of life.

Buddhist meditation teacher Sharon Salzberg notes in her book *Real Love: The Art of Mindful Connection* that "perfectionism is an unproductive use of attention. Self-hatred will not make us better."

When I began to view perfectionism as a form of self-hatred, I could see how deeply it was a violence towards ourselves, running primarily on deep fear. But even more so, I could see that it is a denial of our intrinsic value as human beings and our inherent lovability and belonging.

What does that do to our capacity to be with what is? How can we bear the reality of life when our delusions and masks shatter to pieces? What does this do to our capacity for resiliency?

Self-hatred bred of perfectionism keeps us disconnected from the relationship we have with ourselves. On the other hand, self-compassion combats the vapid perfectionism rampant in our culture at large, and in startup cultures specifically. The essence of love is an undemanding presence in life, in rapport with ourselves at such a level that we have an inner locus of knowing who we are.

Love is not performance; it's presence. And it's not based on your ROI, but on your innate worth as a human. Changing your stance in life—from squeezing into an ill-fitting box of perfection to a more generous stance of love—brings you back to wholeness and fosters a resiliency that's got room for everything life brings you.

OPENING DOORS

No one can make you feel inferior without your consent.

—Eleanor Roosevelt

The feeling of not being enough as we are can result in internal banter as we struggle with deeply held beliefs that hold us captive. Sometimes our many internal narratives can be variations on the theme: Who do you think you are? (Many times, insidious questions of this genre are inflamed by a sense of shame.) Untended to, these can run feral and govern our lives in unruly ways.

Anything that calls into question our enoughness is worthy of deeper exploration so that these thought lines do not pervade our lives. When we doubt our own worth, we lead life from that contracted place. Our lives become confined by this diminishing stance as we allow external narratives about who we are, who we should be, and what's possible for us to have the weight to displace us.

Becoming aware of the internalized messages about how we should be in the world, and locating the beliefs that limit the expansive possibilities available to us because of who we are, is an everyday "fight the good fight" sort of inner wrestle. Beliefs lodge deeply. They constellate with other beliefs in our body-mind-heart complex and create boundaries from which we operate in the world.

> How often do you feel you have the right to be yourself?

> What factors or situations cause you to question the right to be yourself?

> What stories do you live by or have you inherited about the way the world is or what is possible for you?

> How does the belief or feeling that you're not good enough, you don't belong here, or you don't deserve X, Y, or Z feed the motif that keeps you small and disconnected from being fully who you are and from what you really want? What are some scenarios in which you can see this play out in your life?

> Where do those messages come from?

The internalized messages that can shape our sense of self are subtle and social. We learn them in our early conditioning—from our parents, grandparents, caregivers, teachers, and churches. They are often gendered, classist, racist, and misogynistic. We learn them from society and cultural norms. Boys feel it when it comes to expressing their whole selves: Boys don't cry. Don't be a sissy. Girls and women feel it in the conflicting messages they receive about the fine line they need to walk to be in the world judgement-free: Be nice. Don't be a bitch. Don't show weakness. Don't throw like a girl. A person of color or someone from an underrepresented part of the human collective might feel it in the myriad subtle and not-so-subtle ways racial messages play out in life, such as what happens when they're simply walking down the street. In many ways, stepping outside these harsh, pre-defined lines and into the out-of-bounds area of the societal playing field feels unsafe. So we stay within the lines. Limited.

When, where, and how do you claim the fundamental right to be yourself?

When we step out of bounds, to be ourselves fully and shame-lessly, we eschew the prescribed notions that make us feel less than. We begin to find that we are, indeed, enough. We can stand our ground there and may stumble grandly into a sense of inherent belonging.

As humans with a case of not being enough running in our lives, we need to instead internalize messages that attest to our belonging as whole persons: You are okay as you are. You are more than enough. You and your entire story are nothing to feel shame about. Moving to that place takes an inner shift to overcome shame, and it takes a larger helping hand from the bright people in our lives to remind us that we are worthy, talented, and capable—and that we matter. The fundamental right to be yourself precedes any narrative from the external world. You have a right to be here.

While reading Michelle Obama's book *Becoming*, I was particularly struck by how, as her extraordinary journey unfolded, the mantra she would use to quell the voice in her head at each juncture was "Am I good enough? Yes, I am."

It's a power line to keep handy and at the ready whenever that inner voice chimes in to try to warn you of your place, that you're not good enough, and who do you think you are, anyway?

When it comes to claiming the fundamental right to be yourself, it helps to have guides along the way—parents, teachers, mentors, managers, or bosses who are in powerful positions (and positions of power)—who can impact your life in positive yet non-grandiose ways. It doesn't take much to open a door for someone, to believe in them, and to let them know they matter. It could be an introduction that begins the first step of a career or supporting a young adult's passion for the arts. It could start by listening and giving someone the space to share their story and be heard. Small acts can make a big difference in how someone reclaims their story and sense of self, and how they heal from the lies they've been told (or have told themselves) about who they are.

Think back over the course of your life and consider:

> How many people in your life opened doors for you?

> How many doors have you opened for others?

> How often have you supported someone else without taking credit?

> How and where can you see your inherent goodness?

My sense is that the majority of us humans have ingested some external narratives that may still be hampering us. Whenever we hear those messages either told to us or running in our internal dialogue, we need to pause and ask that narrator: According to who or what? In so doing, we call that voice on its malarkey. And from that place, we can begin to include ourselves in our own narrative. That is how we honor and respect our fundamental right to be here.

When in Doubt: Find Your Personal Power

What is your relationship to your own agency, your personal power? When and where do you set it aside? When did you first begin to doubt it? When, where, and how do you exercise it? If you're sitting on a big challenge, issue, or dilemma, notice where your creative agency (your power) is as you think about what's in front of you. Then consider these questions:

> - What is the emotion, the feeling you're having?
> - What information does that feeling have for you?
> - What is happening in your body as you feel into the issue?
> - If there are no words for what you're feeling, what are you sensing?
> - If you were to draw or sketch the feeling, what would the lines look like?
> - What is your gut feeling? If your gut could talk, what would it say?
> - As you look at the issue, check in with your chest, your heart. When do they feel contracted or expansive?
> - What is your instinct? What is the first impulse towards the issue?
> - What feels like a next move, next step? What in you tells you so?

There's a risk in shrinking from our inner knowing. If that habit didn't change, what might you miss out on? How might your world change if you trusted yourself?

SACRED PAUSE

Hurrying and delaying are alike ways of trying to resist the present.

—Alan Watts

As I was leaving the condo this morning, I poked my head into my room as Ginger-the-Wonder-Cat lounged in the sunny spot at the foot of my bed, calmly watching the hubbub happening just outside the window. The roofers were re-roofing the complex with much hammering, thumping, and rattling of the walls inside and out. I wondered if this commotion would rattle her animal nervous system into an over-alert panic, as some things on the outside world can often do.

While her napping continuity may have been disrupted by bumps and thuds from the outside world, her body was devoid of tension. Nonplussed and unbothered, she noticed this new commotion, not hooked or unhinged by it, nor toying with it in the theater of her mind. The scene felt like a brilliant image for what's possible for us humans when we're able to separate our thoughts from our belief in them, and how that drastically affects our ability to have a sense of spaciousness within ourselves and simply notice the world happening on the outside.

One of the greatest things about being human is our ability to change our mind. We can change what we think, and therefore affect how we feel, which in turn may affect our choices and actions. Choices and actions are the two things in life that humans can control. That's it. Over time and with practice I've learned that working with my inner dialogue is part of Contrology 101. The more I can recognize my thoughts as thoughts—like noticing weather patterns yet not getting caught up by them—I am able to see how those thoughts about the outside world lead to story-making that causes my inside world to experience feelings I'd rather not feel.

The mind has the capacity to be The Great Mythmaker, spinning up all kinds of storylines—good, bad, worse, and terrible—that, of course, you can choose to believe, or not. When you do believe certain thoughts or listen to the mythmaker's latest storylines, do you notice what happens to your feelings of stress, anxiety, fear, anger, sadness, joy, or serenity? Depending on what's reeling through my mind, I can feel any of these things. If I follow my thoughts into their weather patterns, it can sometimes feel like I stepped into a tornado of my own making (though I don't always realize it was of my own making). Pretty soon, if I don't come to my own rescue, I can be lathered in mild terror and convinced that my partner is leaving me, I'm not good enough, no one loves me, and the world is ending. Sometimes that's all from interpreting something as provocative as a long time lapse in texting or what someone meant by replying okay.

When you realize you are not your thoughts, that they are things that float in and out of your mind and awareness, you can keep them from taking over your present moment. Here are a few questions to get you started:

> What conversations are you having with yourself?
> What storylines are brewing in your gray matter?
> How are those thoughts affecting your feeling state?
> Are they riling you up, or chilling you out?

When I'm really spinning, especially with my significant other or my business partners, I've learned that revealing the content of my mythmaker helps discharge my mental frenzy, which may be affecting my way of relating to others in my life. I'll identify where I'm at and announce, "I'm having the thought that [insert mythmaker storylines here]." Sometimes it's a relief just to name it. This a) allows me to separate from crazy-making thoughts, and b) gives me the space and perspective to see what's really happening for me and untangle the storylines so I can be here, now, in real time. This simple tool can keep you out of the past and keep the past in the past, so you can be present.

Tending to this field of thoughts is big magic. Herein lies your suffering or your freedom. The conversations you have with yourself directly affect your outlook, your mood, and how you live your life. If you find yourself emotionally distraught or mind-bottled by the mythmaker, remember this: You're not thinking big enough.

If we choose to believe some of the less-than-generative things spinning in our minds, we limit our experience. We also limit our imagination and our sense of what's possible. We forget who we are. For example, if you believe a terrible thought to be true, there are likely a thousand ways in which it is not true. Touching on the neurology for a moment, there are parts of our brain that don't know the difference between imagination and reality, and with no sense of time. In other words, the past is now and the future is now. Therefore, if you imagine something terrible or wonderful, or revisit a memory, you can feel physiological shifts in your body as it watches that scene in the theater of your mind as if it's happening right now. Depending on what programs you have running, and what meaning you're making about those thoughts you're believing, you can make yourself feel better or worse. Most of us are making sh*t up all the time—often about ourselves. And 99.99 percent of it isn't true. That is a violence to ourselves. In that headspace, we're cut off from something life-giving, like the juicy imperative of our inherent goodness.

One of the many gifts of mindfulness is that it sits us down in front of this choice, and gives us space to tend to what we're creating in our lives. So take a sacred pause: Just breathe and notice, without trying to do or fix anything. What is life like right now? What has your attention? Is that adding stress or something generative to your experience?

The sacred pause is a bit like stopping at a red light. It's internalizing your creative agency and taking responsibility for what you're creating in your life. This is the important work. Your practice for how you hold and direct that most important conversation with yourself is what tends to the process of your own becoming. You can lessen the violence to yourself and others by working with your thoughts mindfully. The practice—the pause—reestablishes a connection to self and flows into every interaction so that you create from a full-hearted place of love, not from a contracted headspace of fear.

Back in college, I used to hike the Triple Tree Trail in Bozeman, Montana, every day to sit on the bench up top and look down at the Gallatin Valley. I would go at dawn or dusk when the sky became imbued with pastel hues. I'd often hit the trail mulling over every thought, problem, and issue I had on me, with my feet matching my pacing thoughts. By the time I arrived at the top, heart thumping and breathing heavily, I'd look out at the view perched from a new perspective. From up there, I could think big enough to see what was really true. I'd wonder about all those problems I thought I had. And my body would soften (like my cat Ginger this morning as she noticed the commotion outside the window) and let it go.

A Daily Check-In

The following questions can become the basis of a solid practice of self-reflection and a way to establish a more compassionate relationship with yourself. During the day, find a moment to pause and check in with these prompts:

> How are you?

> What are you feeling? (Name the feelings, or do some expressive doodling on what you're feeling now. What would those feelings look like if they were an image or drawing?)

> What thought patterns do you notice?

> What are three things you are grateful for?

> What can you celebrate?

> How can you rest?

THE GREAT REWILDING

As we bumble through life, trying to figure out who we are as leaders, lovers, parents, and humans, we often get caught up in measuring ourselves against the false requirements put forth by the norm—and we inevitably fall short. In his book *Reboot*, Jerry writes about how so much self-denigration and suffering happens because we create a norm with externally defined standards to live up to. It can feel uncomfortable to be different, to go against that norm in its myriad forms. Yet in the attempt to fit in, we often abandon our true self in all of its wild promise (which ultimately, in the long game, doesn't feel great either).

There's a subtle, yet harrowing, inquiry we ask of ourselves from time to time: Why can't I get it? What's wrong with me that, I'm not like everyone else? Therein lie the brambles we get snared in on the way to finding ourselves. Once we're tangled up like that we put limitations on ourselves and squash what makes us who we are as individuals.

"If you are living for an ideal and driving yourself as hard as you can to be perfect—at your job or as a mother or as a perfect wife—you lose the natural, slow rhythm of life," notes the late, great Jungian analyst Marion Woodman. "There's a rushing, trying to attain the ideal; the slower pace of the beat of the earth, the state where you simply are, is forgotten."

We can give up a lot to fit in. We hand in the fullness of our creative agency. We transfer over our best light and dim the spark that lights us up. When we seek approval from the outside world, we risk giving up our true self. Ultimately, we give away the power that is ours and miss out on allowing the wild part of us to come through.

Gabrielle Roth, in *Maps to Ecstasy: The Healing Power of Movement*, reminds us:

> Where we stopped dancing, singing, being enchanted by stories, or finding comfort in silence is where we have experienced the loss of soul. Dancing, singing, storytelling, and silence are the four universal healing salves.

Early conditioning sets the stage for our future by providing the internalized rules embedded in our psyches about how to live, and how to find (or at least, how our toddler minds feel they need to find) the triad of love, safety, and belonging. Many beliefs and strategies are galvanized at least by age five, and from there forward we can forget our wild self—the self that is humming beneath the wraps of rules and definitions we thought we needed (and perhaps we did in some instances) to get us here. Our wild self is the us that was before we felt pressure to fit into a mold, before we were groomed or had a list of *shoulds* to become. That wild part of us is intimately connected to our true self.

There's so much beauty, difference, and variety lost when we hide or leave aside who we are. If only we felt okay: if we felt safe, if we felt we belonged and were loveable for being exactly who we are. What could *that* new normal look like?

The road to adulthood is littered with opportunities to shrug off old customs, look closely at strategies we've acquired, and question traditions. Along the way, with the firm excavator of some radical self-inquiry, we hone in on the important question of Who am I?

Our wild self isn't feral, crazy, uncontrollable, aggressive, or rabid. It's our preconditioned self, our native self, the "before we were shaped by the world to fit in better" self. That wild self has a boatload of knowing about what we need and what we want and what our aliveness feels like.

How might a mighty human protect that wild promise?

I feel that one must be brave, fierce (not ferocious), honest, in tune and attuned to one's unique hum (the aliveness that buzzes in your veins even before you have caffeine in the morning). One could look at the journey into adulthood as a great rewilding of sorts. And during the many years of midlife is when we recover and integrate that wild part of ourselves more fully, realizing its value and place in this world, and rewriting previous scripts to the contrary.

In her brilliant little book *The Little Girl Who Gave Zero F*cks*, author Amy Charlotte Kean tells the story of a young red-haired Elodie-Rose who lives in a world with a harsh need to change her. She keeps herself strong, centered and unf*ckwithable as she moves through the moments that can throw a young life off-kilter, such as the moods and judgements of others, celebs and trends, boys and teachers. She looks at the world with firm eyes saying, "This is where I stand." Through it all she keeps her basket of f*cks intact, giving them to no one. Where her energy could have been potentially lost by being emotionally entangled in those interactions, it was instead freed up to fuel her dreams. In the process, she finds freedom being herself, shamelessly so.

Giving zero f*cks is the ultimate form of self-respect and a radical act of self-care: we're discerning about where our energy goes, what we choose, and what we focus on—be it in our creative work or any psychic weight we take on or unload. We're firm not only about where we stand but also in sourcing a sense of safety, belonging, and love from an internal reservoir. Here we're not giving away our power and energy to others in order to get or receive something. Instead, we're bringing a sense of security and self-assuredness to our decisions, relationships, and communications.

Second adulthood (aka midlife) is a time of individuating from the ways we are enmeshed with the world, ridding ourselves of ways we get thwarted by patterns of behavior that short-circuit our ability to live out our lives in fullness. We can choose to look closely at what's driving us.

Living according to an internal metric means living in integrity with the fierce fire of your longing, what you know is right, and what is right for you. You can begin that journey here by asking yourself:

> What might it look like to heed and foster this wild promise?

> Where do you let other things supersede the quieter, more subtle, and potent parts of yourself?

> Where do you slip away from the fierce burning of your longing, and what do you settle for instead?

Tending to the sacred fire in your heart is worth keeping at the center of what you do and how you move through your days. Doing so is keeping your wild promise aflame.

THE SOUND OF SETTLING

*The second half of life isn't about looking for easy
answers. It's about honestly exploring the questions
that bring richness and value to your life.*

—James Hollis

"To be an adult is to know what you want and to do it," my therapist said to me at the end of a session one day. Then he added, "Blessed is the person who knows what she wants." There's something subversively simple about his adage about being an adult. How many of us know what we really want and are able to live in concert with our heart's longing, uncluttered by the ways in which the world makes that difficult?

When we step out into work-life—after ingesting what we know about work from our caregivers, our motivations, the ideas that drive us, and what we think we want—we may find ourselves lost and consumed in the fire, or just lost and losing touch with ourselves—or both. Until we walk outside. In her book *If Women Rose Rooted*, psychologist and mythologist Sharon Blackie writes:

> There is a hollow desperation which, from the inside, borders at times on madness in living a life which you know is the wrong life, while not being able to see a way out. When all of your childhood conditioning tells you to stick with it, keep yourself safe, always vote for security and

certainty. But I knew that I was not who I was supposed to be; I knew in my heart that I didn't like my life, and my body was beginning to buckle under the strain.

A founder once noted to me that his bias was always company, company, company. He admits that tactic may not have worked, as a sense of joy felt elusive or vacant. He added that his nightmare was having great professional success and looking in the mirror not being proud of who he saw. There he stands on the precipice of moving into something new and wanting to do it differently, as if there's a deeper voice calling him to question just how to do that since the old way wasn't ultimately as fulfilling as he would like.

In their own way, our trials and tribulations lead us to the juncture at midlife ripe with questions that will inform our second act, that of our second adulthood, the place where we are called to step more into our authenticity and purpose. Midlife is an opportunity to pause and ask the questions that linger and go deep—those that may change the course of our way of being in the world and refine what we are living for, if we're aware enough to heed the call. If we're lucky, we'll pick up on life's messages and listen with another part of us, one that's been with us all this time yet was driven by other motives.

As you reflect on your work, your relationships, and your role in life at this inflection point, something more purposeful emerges—or wants to emerge. Questions arise from a part of you that had been bowled over in pursuit of success according to the world. These questions are quiet but persistent, and the answers seem nostalgically close:

> Who am I, really?

> What am I doing?

> What patterns, programs, and remnants from the past have directed my life?

> What's my work to do in the world?
> What have I lost along the way?
> What do I need to reclaim?
> What would I like in this second act of my life?
> How do I get there?

Discovering clarity in what you'd like moving forward from that place, unpacked from external influences and separated from the images of how you *should* be, is no small task, as it is rife with information gleaned from all of your formidable years. It may require sifting through all that was internalized about how you think you should be and what it even is to be yourself, unfettered by the emotional complexes of whatever you think you can possibly have or even deserve. You have to listen closely to hear the still voice resounding within.

Rumi tells us:

The breeze at dawn has secrets to tell you.
Don't go back to sleep.
You must ask for what you really want.
Don't go back to sleep.

You must ask for what you really want. Perhaps in that line of questioning, we come closer to what Rob Brezsny, in his book *Pronoia*, calls our primal longing: "Your primal longing is the deepest yearning you have; the essential desire that brought you here to earth; the reason why you're alive; the goal that's most important for you to strive for this lifetime; your core driving force."

At first blush, responding to "'What would you like?" and the more soul-resounding undertones of our deepest yearnings can be mired in our sense of self-worth, beliefs about the right to be here and take up space; feelings of guilt or selfishness; subtle unnamed fears of surpassing those who came before us in our family lineages;

and many other meanings we made up about what it means to be safe, to be loved, and to belong. In the midst of all that, we may realize that this may be the first time we've stopped to ask ourselves that question, giving us an opportunity to feel and imagine new possibilities that come from our authentic place in the larger belonging to the world, from a wider view of who we are outside of our roles in life. It's a knowing we have in our bones, versus one we garner as we grow up trying not to be consumed by the world.

Some folks have a sense of the pulse of their core driving force, whereas others forsake it. Many of us feel limited by all our learned ways and the ways in which the world's harsh need to change us has dampened our full range of movement and imagination. In his poem "Second Life," David Whyte calls this our uncourageous life. But there is a first life, a courageous life, offering a different way of being in the world guided by an internal locus that's had us all along.

I felt this distinction in my former marriage, like I was toeing the line between the two worlds. Together, we had a young, driven, and accomplished life and all of the accoutrements informed by our Midwestern roots: the cat, the dog, the house in Boulder, the backyard, the garden, the recreational gear. He worked as an architect at a top firm while I finished my master's degree. We had life well knit together by the looks of it. While I loved parts of our life, I was dying on the inside. While I could have stuck with the relationship (like the women in my lineage before me) and stayed complicit in living a life that wasn't mine, I had to call it in honor of the part of me that knew this wasn't wholly what I wanted.

It was hard to speak what I wanted out from under all those suffocating layers. The band Death Cab for Cutie sang it well in "The Sound of Settling:"

I've got a hunger twisting my stomach into knots
That my tongue has tied off

My brain's repeating, if you've got an impulse, let it out
But they never make it past my mouth

Those words that had a hard time making it past my mouth itched—literally, culminating in a full body rash—until I let them out and ended a six-year relationship. But more importantly, I began a much deeper commitment in the relationship I had to myself by following the truth of my own longing. I didn't know where I was going as there was no map, not like there was for doing the expected adult things like getting mortgages, jobs, and married. I said *yes* to myself and followed the honest wishes of my deep longing.

"Throughout the journey of transformation," my colleague Jim Marsden says, "when we come to a crossroads unsure of which direction to head or which choice to make, if we simply let ourselves sink into the vulnerability that is our deep longing, then an opening presents itself and the next steps become clear."

Being still with that vulnerability is the hardest part, perhaps, because it can be so uncomfortable. Yet when endured, that's where the magic is. Perhaps that's when we learn to meet life and let life meet us. Tapping into that isn't something we can think ourselves into. I had a client at a crossroads recently say, "I have to figure this out!" I prompted, "Maybe this is something you need to *feel* out?"

In other words, perhaps there's another way to be with the longing that may be very present but still have you completely stumped about how to pursue what's next. At the crux between your old life and your new center of gravity, you can begin to see clearly the learned formats that have eclipsed your longing and sense of wonder—your original way of being in the world. Returning to that stance with life can feel contrary to how you have organized yourself in the world for so long.

Work can lead us down a similar path of growth and discernment that is lined with longing and purpose. The traditionally held belief about work—that you find a job in your twenties and work there until you retire—is changing. Startup life and the modern-day trajectory through a career path provide us a not-so-linear opportunity for our own personal development. And if we are to use work as an opportunity for self-actualization, and we view work as a way to do our inner work, we may be given more than one opportunity for our own evolution. Looking at it that way, we can really see how the seasons of our lives mesh with the transitions inherent in startup careers.

No matter where you are in life and work, "What would you dare ask for?" is a good question to keep close and ask often.

Making Joy a Necessity

Maya Angelou told us: "We need joy as we need air." Experiencing joy doesn't make us disloyal to our pain. But a life focused solely on the various sufferings that grace our humanity leaves out the other even more juicy parts of a wholly lived, soulful life. Taking your joy into your own hands not only flexes those neuropathways, it puts you in tune with your aliveness—which has a direct correlation to your creativity.

Start by identifying:

> Big and small, what are the things that bring you joy?

> What do you love to create? What do you love to do?

> How can you let joy be your litmus or barometer so you can lead with joy?

> How can those levels of joy help you determine what you let into your life and what you say no to?

> How can you become more attuned to how this part of your soul is speaking to you?

> What daily life do you want to create?

THE TRUTH ABOUT
WHO YOU ARE

The word *soft* feels important to me. It conjures a wish for the relaxing of mental, emotional, and physical tension—a letting go and letting myself be where I am with things as they are. Mary Oliver's famous line "Let the soft animal of your body love what it loves" from her poem "Wild Geese" crosses my mind often, like the flocks of geese that cross the sky over the barn every winter.

I have been learning to fully trust that line from Oliver's poem as a way to move through life. Lately, this question has become my litmus test: Does the whole of me love this opportunity? There's a deep attunement to how my body responds versus what my mind thinks I want or need. This year, I've been feeling good in work and health and horse realms, finding more moments of peaceful flow in it all. I am in a place I had once longed for, without much notice from anyone but me. In a quiet way, usually when I'm grooming a horse, I remind myself that my well-being is my contribution to life.

Well-being is the state of being comfortable, happy, and healthy. My horses clearly know the world through the "soft animal of their body," and they carry an innate wisdom on this way of being in the world because they so grandly inhabit their body all the time. Their survival depends on being alert to their environment, yet there's an equanimity to their way of being.

Linda Kohanov notes in her book *Power of the Herd: A Non-predatory Approach to Social Intelligence, Leadership, and Innovation,*

"No matter what happens, horses exhibit exceptional emotional agility: they experience each moment openly and authentically, blazing through fear, power, pain, excitement, loss, playfulness, and unmitigated joy. And then they go back to grazing, spending a significant portion of each day milling languidly about in a state of deep peace that arises naturally when you're not afraid of *life*."

When we come to know the life in our body, we arrive at our place in the world. It's a quiet, hard-earned arrival. We have to fight through thickets of thought patterns and mires of fears and feelings to find this place. We have to listen closely to recognize our voice, to sift it out from the obligations and guilt that rush over our needs. Here, we can find ourselves being in the world in a new way, somehow clear and calm despite whatever is happening, inhabiting a place of rest where we cannot mistake ourselves as more graced or graceful than we are.

Embodiment determines our possibilities. How we inhabit our body equates to how we inhabit our lives. We all have ways of dissociating or numbing ourselves. We hide behind masks and makeup and ambitions that aren't in alignment with who we really are. And yet, as poet and essayist Gretel Ehrlich writes in *The Solace of Open Spaces*, "Everything in nature invites us constantly to be what we are." How can we be who we are if we're not at home in the meatsuit that connects us to the magic of being alive?

Full-bodied presence is something horses have in spades. This way of operating through life is the stuff of the oft-quoted ancient sages. With a thousand-plus pounds of horseness that can feel a fly land on them, they can teach us a thing or two about being mindful (versus having a mind full of things like stories about ourselves and the world) and being fully present in our bodies. If you want a mainline to the fruits of meditation, hanging out in a herd of horses is a direct way to awakening your animal body.

As prey animals, equines have a nervous system that's hyper-specific, which means they have an acute sensitivity that can read what's happening on the landscape in a half mile radius around them. Horses can also pick up on emotions and feeling states of herd members. When you are in their presence as part of the herd, they can read you too. In that way, they can help us find congruence in ourselves with who we really are, how we are being, and how our wholeness serves the whole herd.

With horses, their nature invites us constantly to be what we are (as I've witnessed time and time again with clients as they find their place in the herd). The real beauty of this mode of coaching work is that there's no thinking your way through a session. No over-rationalization, rants, story-making, or other forms of verbosity. In the wholeness of the herd, these things are mild liabilities. In this field, you must feel your way through. Your body becomes your guide, just like the way the horses know and move through the world. In a sense, you find your horse body.

Horses show us another way of knowing outside the realm of thinking. We remember ourselves; we discover capacities we didn't realize we had to help us meet life in a new way. Our problems and possibilities look and feel different when we sense them from our horse body.

When you find the soft animal of your body, you're moving outside in the world in accordance with your insides and all the knowing that lies within. As you awaken the larger sensory perception vessel that is your terrestrial meatsuit, you ask different questions from life and you know, deeply, that the only thing life is asking from you is to be who you are. How you are in the world changes. You do not need accolades, compliments, validation, or to be seen in a certain way. A whole lot of psychic energy is freed up in this newfound freedom, when you let the soft animal of your body love what it loves. There's a deep peace there, echoed not only by the wild geese and a herd of horses, but your very soul.

Sometimes I wonder if this equanimous presence is the quality sought after in our hero/ine's journeys. Far from being a disembodied observer of life, we are who we are without letting our thinking get in the way. It's a presence that's in tune with what breezes our skin and stirs within, and it is connected to the larger web of life spontaneously happening in concert along with us.

The greatest gift you can give to anybody is your own well-being. This is in many ways the greatest gift you can offer up to the world, more so than any ambitious plans.

We are often split between wanting to do and be something in the world, to feel our importance in some way, or to just be who we are. As if being who we are belies importance. Perhaps we doubt that who we are is enough. Following our drives to be and do something great can lead us down roads that aren't ours to follow, that aren't congruent with our essence. Who we are is quieter, subtle, and aches for less fanfare than the striving part of us that adheres to shoulds, should nots, and ambitions that anchor our importance. Being and moving through the world fueled by our deepest fears puts our body and soul in a quandary. Most often, we blow right past the wisdom of the body as a guide for moving through the world.

What would it be to move through the world fueled by what we love?

The way of the horse is a potent model for this way of being in the world. A secure, well-adjusted horse senses what is happening and what wants to happen versus fixating on what should and shouldn't happen. He will then decide if what is developing is in his best interest. He'll either go with the flow or get out of the way.

"Your problem is how you are going to spend this one and precious life you have been issued," asserts Anne Lamott in her book *Plan B: Further Thoughts on Faith*. "Whether you're going to spend it trying to look good and creating the illusion that you have power over circumstances, or whether you are going to taste it, enjoy it, and find out the truth about who you are."

Arriving at the ground at our own feet may not be glamorous, but learning to be at home, in our place in space, is gloriously livening. When we choose to inhabit our life, this homecoming becomes inevitable. We stop mistaking ourselves for something we are not. We stop skittering across the surface of our lives.

How Do You Locate Your Inner Knowing?

The soft core of who we are is what is behind all the layers we gather or the shells we adapt into armor (like a hermit crab) to make ourselves feel safe and protected as we move through life. Similarly, while the ego serves a purpose in our life, it's not the whole of us. And when there's a sea change, all that protection doesn't always hold up.

When our ideas of ourselves and the world break against the shoreline, our soft core remains. That soft core is our closest self, a flame of consciousness that's more than just a lifeline. As the terrain, tides, and weather shift around you, something in you knows where to go. Sometimes, the beacon isn't located outside like a distant Polaris. Most often, it's so close we miss it.

Even on the sunniest days when we think we've got the world figured out, we don't ever really know what will happen. But when you feel lost in the ebb and flow on the shoreline of life's circumstances

> How do you know who you are? What tells you that?

> What in you informs you of your deepest knowing?

> How is that knowing part of your resilience?

That, there, is the pulse and flavor of a life fully lived.

L-I-V-I-N

My hut lies in the middle of a dense forest;
Every year the green ivy grows long.
No news of the affairs of men,
Only the occasional song of the woodcutter.
The sun shines and I mend my robe.
When the moon comes out, I read Buddhist poems.
I have nothing to report my friends.
If you want to find the meaning, stop chasing so many things.

—**Ryokan**

Lately, my life feels like the Ryokan lines above. What's in front of me, where my hands and heart and attention currently are, makes my days feel full and intense like a deeper spiral into life. I'm not wishing outward, nor harried to chase things beyond this—except maybe lunch. It's very much a Zen-like attention to the simple tasks of life. This hands-on-world feels ordinary and sacred all at once. It feels whole, connected to the pulse of life and to my pulse within it as I "groom horse, write newsletter." The grounding I feel is borne of a sense of belonging to it all.

When I tune in to the cadence of the summer grass, the sound of my horse's hooves on the earth, the evening's cool mountain air blowing down from the foothills, the twinkle of the stars, the sound of crickets and the flickering city lights far in the distance, I find my place in space. That place where I am part of a larger symphony playing out all around me. It may seem like there's nothing to write home about here, yet there's so much richness that can't be captured on film or in pixels. Something different happens here. Meaning hangs in these moments. Far, far away from "likes" and "loves" and giving a rat's arse what other people think, I find myself feeling "This is *it*."

This is how my horse knows life. In tune with the wind, the wild and lonely sky, the birds, the bugs, the barn cat. His whole way of being in the world is wired to sense the rhythm of things great and small, at great distances as well as close in. He can even feel how I am feeling. He knows that we're not just *on* the brink of everything, we're *in* the brink of everything on the brink of everything. If I get still, I can feel the rustle and hum of my place within it all, like he can.

Our life is ours to be lived. There's no external measure of worth that determines our inherent deservingness of what is ours. Yet sometimes we get that backwards. We are all too often hooked on outcomes. We measure how many steps we take, how many likes we have, what certifications we've achieved, how many prizes we've won, how many zeros in our net worth. Somehow gaining those things aims to bolster our sense of self-worth. But what's missing? How is "chasing so many things," as Ryokan commands us, generative and life-giving?

What would happen if we made choices that take into account our *aliveness factor*? (Versus choices that deny that, in lieu of something that looks more like the mythical "up and to the right" lifepath?)

A big switch from measuring to meaning (or perhaps "from misery to meaning," to borrow a line from James Hollis) happens in our way of being when we open up to what's here with us all the time. When we can find our presence—which is subtle and resounding all at once—we can sense the bigness holding us, something missed as we buzz through life tangled in our thoughts and patterns and Instagram accounts. In turn, we lighten the load of all that measuring that takes a toll on our posture and lifeforce.

(Insert a deep breath here.)

(And another one if you need it.)

When we arrive here, we find ourselves oriented differently. Here, the sound of crickets may be a welcome recognition of homecoming versus an anxiety-inducing silence. Here, there's a different rhythm to march to—one commanded from inside us. If we heed that rhythm, what's dormant or dry within us might enliven and spark. Without tuning in to this subtle and important part of ourselves, we can become rigid in mind and body, aching and pained, distant from our deepest longings. We may find our heart has been empty all this time. If we can touch into, even briefly, the sense of miracle and wonder (something we may have lost along the way since we were little humans), we may interrupt fixed ways of thinking that hold us tight and hold us back from our own fulfillment.

The question that's been holding my attention these days is: If I was going to die tomorrow, what would I do right now? This prompt proves to be a blade of clarity. Will I lean into my aliveness? Will I follow the trail of shoulds? It helps me find my place in space again and align with how I want to live my life.

What if we stopped chasing so many things? There is a constant no matter where we stand: we've already arrived. There's no "out there" to be achieved or attained. Here we are. From here the questions become: How have I lived? How am I living?

THE ONLY LIFE YOU
COULD SAVE

At least once a week, an inquiry comes through our website from someone wanting to discover or connect with purpose, usually with the subtle tonality of heart-aching longing. Finding purpose and meaning in our lives becomes paramount when it comes to our work and how we endeavor to make a living.

For a lot of folks, their work has nothing to do with their purpose. I feared being in that position when I was younger. I watched my dad, who always wanted to be a history teacher, slog it out at his sales job and then come home and immerse himself in old war histories, stories about the space program, and everything Ken Burns created. I watched his heart's desires clash with his practical "I must make money and provide for my family" sense of duty, and vowed never to put my heart and purpose in that kind of peril.

I'm here for a reason, and I knew it. I wasn't letting my dream get away from me. Nor was I going to let a way to make a living get in the way of me actualizing it. My inner meter for soul-sucking was a highly sensitive instrument.

We get closer and closer to purpose when we begin bringing forth our most authentic self. That is the task of a lifetime, with no clear-cut linear process. There's no way to hack that one by doing steps A, B, C, etc., and then saving one morning a week for journaling with a liter of bulletproof coffee. Unfolding your authentic self has its own rhythm in accordance with you and all the baggage with which you were fated and imprinted. To top it off, emerging often requires some kind of fire, the way a mesquite tree needs that intense heat to grow, or the alchemist's crucible turned lead into gold. How many of us are willing to go there? How many of us stop short, just before it gets uncomfortable? Or how many of us rush past the keys that could open us to our purpose?

Back in the day, I used to work with people on bringing their work into the world. My work felt akin to being a midwife for other people's creations. At first, I thought of this as an innocent task. I quickly learned that the edge of what we want to bring into the world the most runs headlong into who we are and the baggage we have. There's a lot of stuff at that edge, usually running with a live wire of fear that can come from a myriad of places and forces—both seen and unseen. Oh hello, subconscious.

It's an interesting edge to meet. You'll likely find your wired safety mechanisms and those voices in your head shouting warnings at you against the change, telling you that if you do change from keeping yourself small, you'll be hurt, unloved, or banished from the tribe. It shows up as resistance, or avoidance, or not really doing our Big Work. Instead, we lead little, safe, mild-mannered lives that don't touch near that livewire edge of fear.

The inner tension between the older parts of ourselves who set up some limiting beliefs between gestation and six-ish years old often need an update on who we are now and how we survived and thrived beyond when our coping mechanisms were put into place. Otherwise, they act out in ways that cloud our clearest purpose. Who do we really want to see/hear/love us? And what do we want them to see? And how old is the version of us that needs that? It's a strange internal battle: reminding those younger parts of ourselves to update their long-held beliefs and fears.

Bringing forth your most authentic self is hard, because it requires that you uncover and face old patterns, imprints from childhood, and all the subconscious things haunting and running your life. It's kinda scary because your most authentic self is that part of you that you had to contain as a young one, to fiercely protect, in order to fit in, be loved, and survive. So you grow up with all that and keep your innate gold under wraps. Along the way, your fated situation in life and the trials and tribulations that you overcome shape you in meaningful ways and become part of what makes this journey all the more...er, arduous and mystifying.

But don't let the mystery or the hard spots, or anyone or anything, stop you. In the grand excavation of you, the other side is worth it—it's full of freedom to be who you are with none of the aforementioned scary loyalties of your subconscious holding you back. True adulthood is a hard-won and beautiful thing.

Yet it's hard to sift through the external voices touting advice, the vapidity on social media, life and job hacking how-tos, your feelings of FOMO, and all the self-doubt and inadequacy you have about yourself and your innate lovability (and all the havoc *that* wreaks). It's a quagmire to find your inner voice, and that's all part of the journey. *Your* journey.

> When was the last time you heard your voice clearly?

> What was happening then?

> How did you recognize that clear voice?

> How do you stay in dialogue with that voice today?

> What do you do to stay connected with and aligned with that voice?

We're all victims of our limiting beliefs. That is a hard-earned edge to inquire about and change. If we don't cross the line to our larger work in the world, or we stifle it with our fears, we snooze through life. (Nobody wants that!) The redeeming moment is when you decide to take your power back and save the only life you can save—your own.

Part III

FROM FEAR TO COURAGE

THE THING ABOUT
HARD THINGS

When difficult things happen, we may not have faith that our insides—our inner landscape, the core faculties of our psyche—know what to do. (Ugh.) That's often when we feel the need to reach for help from the pages on a shelf, or a post on the internet, or the latest podcast on the topic related to our situation. Some of us search for the playbook—the definitive What to Do. But not everything, despite the claims, can be a one-size-fits-all solution. In fact, few things are.

There's no shortage of hard things we'll encounter in our lifetimes and our own arcs of personal growth as humans. Sad things that leave us grieving. Changes that make us angry. Events that make us feel helpless or scared or stuck. A year like 2020 comes along and knocks everything off the table, or feels like a game of 52 Pickup in a hurricane. All these external events strike the internal emotional chords that inform our own experiences. So how do we respond?

Sometimes when hard things happen, or when things feel hard, it can be most useful to reach inside for the core of who you are and just notice what is happening there:

> Where is your attention?

> How activated is your nervous system?

> What are the sensations in your body?

> What thoughts are you having?

> How is your breath?

Gentle inquiry like this can be an anchor when the going gets rough, when your palms feel sweaty, or when your heart feels broken. Such an inquiry can lead you to your core—that intact part of you that knows important things such as:

> What does this remind you of?

> What might you need right now?

> What does your gut say?

> What is your impulse for a next step?

> What potential choice makes you contract?

> What potential choice feels like a clear yes?

GETTING CURIOUS

The self which he has believed himself to be, is nothing but a pattern of habits or artificial reactions.

—Alan Watts

As humans, our multilayered neural complexities run many programs that ultimately define numerous patterns as we go about our lives. Some of these programs may feel so innately part of us that we issue statements like "This is who I am" as if it's a fixed state. Our deeply ingrained patterns or habits can take over our lives; they can make change a struggle or keep us from realizing our potential to achieve what we'd like. It takes a savvy awareness to recognize that who you think you are may be merely, as Alan Watts writes, "a pattern of habits or artificial reactions." Ultimately, you are not what you think.

So much of what we do on any given day is a result of behavioral programs deeply encoded in our individual wiring. If we really looked at all the information that makes up something as seemingly benign as a decision we make, if we could review our human neurology structures like we analyze lines of code, we might see how much old code commands inform our current choices, actions, and the places where we get stuck.

Sorting out our behaviors can shed light on our way of being in the world and how we can move forward with more clarity and grace. As coaches, we deal with change—and the wish for change—as part of our work with clients. Change can be hard. Shifting any cycle in which we get stuck takes conscious effort to bring awareness about what's really happening in those moments so we can meet life fully, free from the defenses that keep us trapped.

Judson Brewer, author of *The Craving Mind: From Cigarettes to Smartphones to Love—Why We Get Hooked and How We Can Break Bad Habits* and director of research at the Center for Mindfulness, has developed novel mindfulness programs for habit change based on findings from numerous studies he and his team have conducted. They investigated the mechanisms for change and how mindfulness acts in our brains in the face of breaking habits, cravings, addictions, cyclical thought patterns, and the things we find ourselves uncontrollably repeating. His research has made me think about how we can work with our brains to overcome the behavioral patterns in our lives that we may not typically classify as a "bad habit." Understanding the inner workings of what's at play in our brains when working to shift our patterns and habits can move us from fear to flow. From there, we can increase our ability to meet life, or let it meet us, in an intimacy-with-all-things kind of way.

Addictions and ego-driven behaviors are self-reflexive in that they are self-referential. Both can consume us before we even know it, much like a psychological complex running an old pattern formed out of a past experience. When we're concerned with our self in this way, a different part of our brain lights up—the part that's identifying with what's happening. When we're in that space, it's all about *me* as a separate entity from the rest of the world (i.e., "I am here and you are out there, but I'm not really concerned about you because I'm too focused on me right now.").

In a January 2018 Reboot podcast episode, Dr. Brewer explained the locations of the brain and what causes those parts to light up:

The medial prefrontal cortex is involved in the conceptual self. Like I wake up in the morning and I remember my name and I remember I have to go to work and I remember where work is, and all those things. Then there's the experiential self, which is the posterior cingulate cortex (or PCC). The PCC registers this contraction that says, "Oh yes, that's me." And this gets activated during a number of different types of tasks. So, for example, when we're thinking about ourselves it gets activated. When we're feeling guilty, it gets activated. When we're emoting about things, when we're ruminating about things, when we're anxious, it gets activated. When we're craving a number of different substances it gets activated. This brain region seems to be activated when we're contracting down around something. The posterior cingulate, on the other hand, gets really quiet when somebody's out of their own way.

Addictions, including addictions to our emotional states, make change challenging. At one of Reboot's bootcamps, a member of the cohort said, "I feel so anxious and depressed. I feel this way so much that I think there's a part of me that's addicted to feeling this way." Our brain gets hooked on a feeling, which in turn affects our behavior in ways not always helpful or healthy for us.

No doubt the strategies we run as humans are crafty—so crafty that if we cave to them unwittingly, we may never get where we want to get. We exhibit the same behavior that sea slugs do: we move towards what feels good and move away from what doesn't. Sophisticated, eh? We're slightly more complex neurologically than sea slugs, in that what feels good or bad to us may have many layers of emotion and meaning attached.

Consider, for example, the artist who's been trying to finish a big piece. Once again, he just can't seem to finish, but goes out to buy more materials and doesn't return to his studio for a while. One might look at that and think, "He was tired, artist-blocked, needed a change of scenery." *He* may even think that himself. Yet looking under the hood a bit, we'll find that as he's getting close to finishing his project, he hears his father's voice saying he'll never amount to anything. That prompts such a cascade of feelings, none of which feel positive, that even the magnitude of joy and satisfaction of possible project completion doesn't exceed that. Our artist contracts down around that moment; he gets stuck there and can't get out.

That one negative-feeling memory snippet can trigger a tense and stressed or anxious feeling, and create the wish for something outside oneself to take the edge off. In this example, the artist decides to run to the store for more supplies. When feelings get too negative, we block them with something else from the outside world (take your pick of addictions: alcohol, food, exercise, video games, work, perfectionism, Netflix, social media, etc.). Often, the less-than-positive feelings are rooted in fear (which at the core is when being loved, belonging, and being safe are threatened). We become deeply concerned about our self.

This fear is an interesting thing to track. In fear, we feel our very breathing, pulsing existence threatened, thus it puts us in a state of self-preservation. Horses exhibit this wonderfully. When my horse is curious, he'll willingly move towards something. When he's afraid of something, he contracts away from it (in his mind, to save his life), and he's incredibly worried. When he's curious, he learns quickly. As the late legendary horseman Tom Dorrance would say, "It doesn't take a lot when it's a learning process and not a worrying process."

It's similar with humans. A worried human is preoccupied and self-identified, wandering in their life thinking, "Am I okay? Do they like me? Am I good enough?" Or we tend to run any version of self-doubt and inadequacy self-talk while varying feelings of insecurity, anxiety, guilt, and self-loathing creep in close behind—all of which from the same place: fear.

"From a survival perspective, fear causes us to contract down into the smallest ball possible to protect our vital organs," Dr. Brewer reminds us. "When we're contracted around some identification with something—like my company or my company's name or whatever—that literally may be the experience in the experiential self because it defines the boundary between myself and the rest of the world."

Think about what happens when you're scared. Depending on what's inducing the fear, you may let your instincts react. Or you get anxiously mind-bottled in trains of terrifying (however unlikely) thoughts that can't derail themselves but keep you spiraling deeper and deeper into the vortex of self-contained, self-reflexive smallness—the world where you're only concerned about *I* and thinking about survival.

Contrast that with other experiences in which you're losing track of time, deep into creative projects and forgetting about lunch because what's happening is so juicy and you're just in it. That's a more expansive place, right? Your sense of self is present and not giving two sh*ts about anything your mind was noshing on as it was swirling into the vortex of fear in the paragraphs above. Odds are good you're super relaxed and not trying too hard to do anything; it's just all flowing with ease. Thinking too hard can get in the way. (I've ruined many a canvas, and many a ride on my horse, by thinking too hard about it.)

When we're in flow, when we're present in the here and now, the "I" that lights up our PCC disappears. When that connection in the brain is strong enough, one feels selfless, being feels effortless, the moment feels timeless, and there's immense joy. There's no survival thinking taking that connection offline into fear and worry mode.

The subversively simple ancient technology of mindfulness gives us the antidote to the patterns that keep us from meeting life fully. It starts with getting curious, which is a choice we have on hand wherever we go. We don't have to check Facebook or email, or reach for something outside of ourselves to feel better. When you notice and get curious, you move from being in your head to an embodied wisdom, which helps the brain rewire. "It also teaches us something really critical," Dr. Brewer notes. "There's a different type of reward that's always available when we move from a contracted 'I have to get something in order to feel better' to an expanded curiosity right in that moment. *Always available.*"

AFTERMATH

I'm always a bit shocked when I hear the infamous statistic that "90 percent of startups fail." The beginning of any entrepreneurial endeavor can seem like a good idea at the time. Do we ever see failure coming? With all the growth and growing pains, influxes of capital, decisions upon decisions, and general entrepreneurial delusions, is there a feeling of failure that we try to avoid? What happens if we don't realize the full potential of the company? What happens when the doors close in front of us?

When the end comes (of anything really—a company, your position, a relationship), it doesn't seem to matter how prepared you were for the final verdict. The traffic of thoughts in your mind can reel between "It's over" and "It can't be over." There's often a plaintive gasp: "It wasn't supposed to happen that way." You rewind memories that retrace the past steps leading to now, and mutter preferred cuss words at all the wrong turns: If only I'd done this, that, or the other, I'd still be in the game. We'd have succeeded if only... As if things could be fixed retroactively through the rear-view mirror. Other thoughts can spiral into a whirling vortex of self-doubt, inadequacy, loathing, and loss. It can seem as if reality shows up swiftly, and so radically different from where we thought we were and where we wanted to end up.

Pema Chödrön writes in *When Things Fall Apart: Heart Advice for Difficult Times:*

Things falling apart is a kind of testing and also a kind of healing. We think that the point is to pass the test or to overcome the problem, but the truth is that things don't really get solved. They come together and they fall apart. Then they come together again and fall apart again. It's just like that. The healing comes from letting there be room for all of this to happen: room for grief, for relief, for misery, for joy.

How can we make room for all of it—what's happened, what's happening now, and the rush of feelings in us? How can we learn to be okay with how things did unfold? How can we relax our "aftermathing" (crunching the numbers, how-comes, whys, and coulda-beens) in the wake of the outcome? How can we find peace with what just went down, and with what is?

The key in times like this, acceptance is the first step. Said Reboot-ily: If this is so, so what? Resisting, fighting, and denying what has happened keeps us from a more easeful flow, and instead keeps us holding up a wall in front of us that increases our struggle. So much of our tension can be released by including all of our experience through the act of acceptance.

Acceptance, a key quality of resilience, is also at the core of mindfulness, which "teaches us the ultimate resilience—to trust in our capacity to wisely and compassionately meet whatever comes our way," as therapist and author Linda Graham notes in her book *Bouncing Back: Rewiring Your Brain for Maximum Resilience and Well-Being*. "Mindfulness—the steady, non-judgmental awareness and acceptance of experience—leads to self-awareness and to shifts in our perspectives that allow us to see clearly what's happening and how we are reacting, to respond to triggers and traumas with far more open-mindedness, and to face the process of necessary change with far more flexibility and tolerance." Together with empathy—"a wholesome practice of connection and acceptance that expands our awareness of resources we can draw on, both within ourselves and from others"—we begin to see the hallmark qualities of emerging resiliency.

Employing both mindfulness and empathy will help us along in the acceptance department. Here, we work to recover our own resilience in those moments when we find ourselves mentally aftermathing scenario calculations that we can't retroactively fix. We can breathe with what is—right now—and make room for everything. And in so doing, we can find a sense of peace that allows us to gather up our inner resources and move on unencumbered from the past and make fresh choices for the future. In other words, if we remain stuck in the quagmire of what we wish would have happened, we limit our capacity to move beyond it, and therefore limit ourselves.

Acceptance allows us to honor and accept an entire event and integrate it into our sense of self—no blame and shame allowed. We must come to understand the narrative of what happened, what we did to survive it, what the cost of that survival may have been, what we learned and can bring forward with us, and how we'd like to respond to life now. What resources can we rely on as we move forward now that we've parsed the equation from this aftermath?

Being able to move through these steps, with the matter-of-factness as if you were reading the back of a box of cereal, involves compassionately meeting not only whatever comes your way but compassionately meeting yourself. That is an act of acceptance and inclusion that is befriending and gentle and present.

Self-acceptance fortifies your emotional foundation to endure what happens so you can enhance your capacity to handle the detours, plot twists, and uncertainty of what's next in life and work. And in so doing, even in the aftermath, you connect with your truest self—a place of inherent goodness, a place that exists in the background of the post-event aftermathing figurations. Catching yourself, and returning to that place, steels you in a way, because you know you can return home there when the going goes haywire.

Resiliency is the ability to overcome all kinds of challenges—trauma, tragedy, personal crises, all the stuff life throws at you—and bounce back stronger, wiser, and more personally fortified. There's something alchemical about it: taking everything you experience and transforming it into something useful.

When I think of resiliency, I think of the ability to show up every day and be present for what shows up to meet me. In the ups and downs of startup life, this is a turbulent adventure we've chosen to embark upon. It's a wild ride with as many unsuspecting blows as there are boons. A client once said to me, "Some days I tell myself I need to get back up on my horse and keep going. Sometimes that's really hard." It takes courage and grit to keep on like that and to face everything as it comes. It requires the capacity to cut through your own tendency for self-delusion and the ability to pick yourself up and harvest all the useful information the experience has given you. The art of resilience allows you to be transformed by the experiences so that you emerge as a truer expression of yourself.

RISKING SIGNIFICANCE

When we open ourselves up to the danger and risk of actually living in a way that is congruent, we naturally live into purpose.

—Jerry Colonna

What does it mean to have a meaningful life?

An interesting question to pose to a human being, also known as a meaning-making machine, in a world that can seem meaningless without our making sense of it. We want significance, purpose, and something worthwhile. (What else?) Double-click into the meaning behind these words for a moment: We want a life that's significant, how? Purposeful, how? Worthwhile, how? And according to whom?

If we are not making up a meaning that feels true to our unique fingerprint and worthy of the pulse of our very own gift of this one life, then we'll likely subscribe to *The Ten Things You Must Do for a Meaningful Life* list that's likely floating around on some life-hacking site somewhere.

When we bump up against our cubicles, commutes, and time clocks with the question of meaning stirring in our head, it's easy to wonder: "Is this all there is?" We long to have more impact. (Who *doesn't* want to be one of those people who makes an impact?) Maybe we long for the promise that there's a better something in the greener fields of the hip interwebs of entrepreneurship. Maybe we long for a life's work that's truly our own, not what our parents wanted. Maybe we hear that line by Annie Dillard in *The Writing*

Life, on repeat tauntingly in our heart-mind, "How you spend your days is how you live your life," or the classic poet Mary Oliver line, "What will you do with your one wild and precious life?" And we say quietly to ourselves, "OMG, WTF am I doing? I need more… *meaning.*"

We set out on that mission. But do we know what we're looking for? How do we go about finding it? All we know is that we don't want to die an unlived life. Are we still barely breathing (and calling it a life) or just breathing twice as fast (and calling it a life) as we check off *The Ten Things You Must Do for a Meaningful Life*?

"The meaning of life is just to be alive," says Alan Watts in *The Culture of Counter Culture.* "It is so plain and so obvious and so simple. And yet, everybody rushes around in a great panic as if it were necessary to achieve something beyond themselves."

There's nothing wrong with the impulse to find meaning. We are meaning-making machines, after all, and living a good life is a key component of living well. But who and what is part of our drive for meaning? How do we define that for ourselves? And what might we be missing in the hunt out of fear of an unlived life?

For some, it's material things—cars, fancy stuff, yachts. For others, meaning is made via some sense of a spiritual life punctuated with lifestyle shifts: collecting malas, tracking our meditation times and fitness routines, consuming superfoods. All are part of the search for meaning via external things, just with different flavors. But have we merely swapped out the things that gratify and validate our ego in a move towards spiritual materialism? Have we begun to use spiritual teachings to build up a limited sense of self or for a sense of false security and comfort—instead of doing the hard work of confronting reality and its impermanence?

In our search for meaning, our suspicions should rise around the things that make us feel secure and comfortable in our knowing of how the world is, the meaning we make around that assumption, and the "Therefore, this is how we are" conclusions we make. We, too, are in flux with the changing nature of reality. Our ego can build up and cling to a sense of self that's relatively fixed. Whenever the ego is involved, fear is present, and it keeps us struggling to be present. Our identification with the fixed self can prevent us from seeing anything but the fluid nature of who we are versus how we construct our lives. How do we build capacity to handle all that flux?

When we stop breathing, we know our fear is taking hold. We contract, we limit our reference point for experiencing life, we look to control things (and create security), and strategize our plans and next bold moves from a scarce place of limited resources.

The ego struggles with the ever-changing nature of reality and the world we live in. It plots, plans, and looks for life hacks to ward off our fear of dying, both materially (as in our body dies) and in significance (when our sense of self that we keep defended and validated is deflated). The ego fears exactly what D. H. Lawrence asks us to do: "Are you willing to be sponged out, erased, canceled, made nothing?…If not, you will never really change."

Can you see how a life with chartable data and a series of predictable if/then rubrics—those that follow a direct path to somewhere up and to the right on the graph—would ease the anxiety caused by the ego's fear of death? If only life could be measured quantitatively or by checklists, we could manage all that uncertainty and maintain our sense of self, right? Instead, we'll optimize to get to the perfect place or state of mind or level of living that's out there (as if that place exists) at 2x speed. Maybe along the way, we could even avoid the suffering inherent in being a sentient being.

And we'll be breathless as we do it. Because we won't be touching on the deeper ache, the deeper longing that's still there—the longing to be present for our life. To be fully alive in the full-spectrum range of experiences a sentient human can handle—the love, sadness, anger, grief, joy, that tingly feeling of aliveness—is it. The work of our lives is to be with life as it happens.

What's happening *is* your life. There's no metric for that. There's no data set or pattern to track to see what's around the next corner. Relying on quantifiable things is delaying the present; doing them faster rushes through it. Our work is to find the space to be with all of it. To be in it. To meet it bravely. To risk our significance, as our ego trembles in fear.

This is the work of your life.

COMPARISON STEALS JOY: TRACKING YOUR PERSONAL RECORDS

When we're worried about happenings outside the boundaries of our own organizations, it detracts from our focus on what's important and what's needed to show up and do the work that is ours to do.

The antidote? Swim in your own lane. Look ahead, take up your space, and worry not so much what others are doing outside your lane marker. Doing so helps us distinguish the noise from the signal.

> What do we need to pay attention to?

> What's the work in front of us?

> What do we know about what we know about?

> What about the known-unknowns and unknown-unknowns?

> What are we sensing from our environments, from our data?

> What is emergent?

> What is our next move from here?

What happens where spirit meets bone, where our insides meet the world at the edges of our meatsuit, is where things get interesting. When you focus your attention there, what happens for you?

The metric that matters in life is your personal best. Being a better version of yourself than you were yesterday, or last month, or than you were in the last five years is growth. In your organization, what matters is your personal best in the collective sense: Month-over-month, year-over-year growth, and tracking your metrics and data give you the visibility you need to understand the drivers of your business. If a competitor's multibillion-dollar valuation has captured your attention like fly tape, then you're swimming in the wrong lane.

UNFOLDING

You need only claim the events of your life to make yourself yours. When you truly possess all you have been and done, which may take some time, you are fierce with reality.

—Florida Scott-Maxwell

Many moons ago, I cried in my undergraduate professor's office at Montana State University after she asked me facetiously, yet seriously, "What do you want to do when you grow up?" That question plagued me from grade school through college, and even after graduate school. I had so many loves and strengths that didn't seem to fit into conventional nine to five options at the time. My Meyers-Briggs© assessment didn't help much either. Being a student in religious studies, I glibly responded to her question a bit like Job: "What does God want me to do?"

Whether divine intervention descended on me or not, I really wanted someone to tell me what I was good at and where I belonged at the intersection of work, purpose, and meaning.

I wanted that more than anything. If I had known there was a place for me to be *me* and be paid for it, I wouldn't have to stick my dreams in a drawer and get a job that could pay for them on the side. The tension between what I really wanted to do, which felt like creativity and freedom, and the pressure I felt to do what I needed to do to pay bills and be a "responsible adult" made me feel like my heart was in a vice.

My Midwest work ethic didn't seem to help. I could do a lot of things well, knew how to get sh*t done, and often took on jobs that weren't leveraging the best of me. The passions I wanted to pour my life into felt like positions that only the luckiest among us get to have. *National Geographic* photographer. Adventure writer. Deep ecologist. Horse whisperer. If I entertained those daydreams for too long, a voice in my head (which sounded a lot like my father, and perhaps the lineage of folks who came before him) said, "Get a real job." Yet the idea of a "real job" crushed my soul to tears. The Wisconsin-raised part of me felt like that was the only option for fiscal sustainability. But when I tried to fit into one of those real job gigs, even though I could do the job better than most folks in the running, a big part of me was dying.

Like many, my career path was a spaghetti line of opportunities and choices. Out of graduate school, I had to find a job with just enough steady income—but more flexibility than the nine-to-fivers to soothe my rebel-heart. So I became a freelance consultant where learned to live life without the benefits granted by a traditional workplace (not that I'd ever experienced them prior to that). Being okay with that level of fluctuating insecurity primed me for working at a startup, and I learned that those benefits weren't necessarily all they were cracked up to be. They certainly didn't outweigh the feeling that my soul was going through a paper shredder on a daily basis.

For some of us, we follow somewhat straighter lines when it comes to work. Our studies match the field we end up in, and we follow jobs in that area. And then at midlife, we find ourselves looking around wondering, "What happened? How did I get here?"

Recently, a client came to me in the midst of sensing transitions in her life. "I'm realizing that I followed this path from college to working in my field, and the job doesn't really care about me," she said. "I want to venture out into something new, and I want the confidence to do it my way because I don't think the prescriptive way works."

Around forty, many of us begin to unpack ourselves from the boxes we've folded ourselves into, especially as it relates to who we are and our work. Many of us arrive here as fine pieces of origami. The existential questions that arise at this time in life are at the intersection of life and work and meaning, and are close to the bone of purpose. They echo and reverberate around Who am I? Where am I? What have I given up? What do I really want?

We ask ourselves many things at this point, among them: How can I be me? and How can I be successful? (as if we have to choose just one). We struggle with the burdens implicit in the questions we ask around being a good provider, being a good partner, providing stability, and having a career on top of everything else that we do. (Can you hear the external reference point of *who* determines if we're measuring up in these questions, as if there's an external standard we're being held to, and the locus of the answers lies outside us?) When did we learn that the only way to be in the world was to fit and form ourselves into a pre-cut notion of who we need to be?

Somewhere along the way, in the map of our body and psyche, we forget that we have the right to be here as we are and to be met by the world as we are. This gets buried by subverted notions of love and belonging that are tied to a world in which we are loved conditionally. No wonder we long for a Strengths Finder© test to tell us what we are.

Perhaps the better set of questioning is: What am I made of? What are the aspects of me? And how do those aspects come together in ways that I am proud of and ways that hold me back?

Those are the questions that honor our wholeness—who we are in totality in our very own life, not merely the results of a series of multiple-choice questions and algorithms. We are more complete, complex, and complicated than any assessment.

Thus begins our unfolding. Eventually, we may arrive and allow ourselves to design our life according to our own creative agency.

Anthropologist and author Mary Catherine Bateson said in an October 2015 episode of *On Being*, "I like to think of men and women as artists of their own lives, working with what comes to hand through accident or talent, to compose and recompose a pattern in time that expresses who they are and what they believe in, making meaning even as they are studying and working and raising children, creating and recreating themselves."

Find some space to pause, and take time to reflect on the following questions:

> How do you set out into life with all of who you are—and trust that?

> Who are you without the tensions and stressors and anxiety you carry?

> Who are you outside of the roles you play in life?

> What is the story you hold of the world that makes you file parts of yourself down so you fit more neatly?

> What would you lose if you lost the box you've fit and formed yourself into?

> What would happen if you became yourself in an unpackaged, unprocessed form?

> What would it feel like to be you, fully?

As you set out to create your life, the best thing you can bring with you is all that you're made of—this is the foundation of your resiliency. Nobody knows the choices you should make, but if you make decisions from a place of connection to yourself and your truth, moment to moment, your choices will match the rhythm of the you that's emerging.

WHEREVER YOU GO

If we hope to go anywhere or develop ourselves in any way, we can only step from where we are standing. If we don't really know where we are standing...We may only go in circles.

—Jon Kabat-Zinn

A handful of years ago, long before Reboot, work felt undeniably crappy. My health wasn't great and the doctors kept saying it was just stress. I would come home after work and lie on my floor; that's all I had left in me. My single-hood had me down too. So I booked a trip to Spain for a wedding. I was excited to leave everything—the work yuck, the stress, the un-enlivened spark that was barely flickering in me—and venture east for fresh sights to feed my weakening body and soul. I hoped, too, that I'd also meet Mr. McDreamy there, have a reason to stay, and leave the rest behind.

That plan sounded good at the time. While I had a good adventure overseas, the trip yielded none of the hoped-for results. I returned home in the same state—or worse, since my feet were sore from walking all over Barcelona (mainly by myself).

I left wanting to get myself out of the cage I found myself in. Instead, it was the perfect example of "Wherever you go, there you are." While I didn't want to pack those messy parts along with me, they came anyway, persistently demanding inclusion. I couldn't separate all that I was feeling, all that seemed so messy about being human at that point in life, from...me. Or as author and mindfulness advocate Jon Kabat-Zinn says, I didn't know where I was standing, so I didn't know where I was stepping from. Hence, I found myself going in circles.

This pattern inevitably shows up in our own lives when the moves we make to change up the lackluster norm and do something different find us not moving too far from what we wanted changed. It can feel like an M. C. Escher sketch of staircases that are going neither up nor down as you traverse them round and round and round. We see this clearly when we leave one job, for good reasons, and find similar scenarios following us into our next gig. It's like we're in another dimension. Or perhaps we're missing a dimension.

We must know where we are standing—*really* know all that's going on inside us in this place in space—for real transformation to happen. Cognitively knowing and understanding your situation, implementing quick fixes, or finding the best way to transition out of a role and into another (insert the awful self-help *Ten Best Ways To...* headline here) doesn't usually change much in the long run. These are superficial layers in any situation; they are the results, not the cause. Diving into your relationship with yourself is when things really start to shift. Those who live and seek one- and two-dimensional answers to life are missing out on a huge opportunity. Dig a little deeper, and you'll find something more fulfilling: what this life is asking of you and how that will fill you up in ways the latest buzz on the internet simply cannot touch.

One night at dinner, I talked with Jerry about why we keep circling around in our stuff, even as we try to change. He offered this perspective:

> Those who look at only one or two dimensions in their life are going to fail to execute that deeply desired trans-formation because they will fail to appreciate the messiness of human beings. You have to look to the Venn diagram of the entire self. Often, we look at the external self first,

with questions like, "Where am I working? How am I working? What are the conditions in which I'm working?" This initial examination occurs without looking at either our soul—with questions such as "Who am I? How have I been formed? What are my beliefs about the world?"—or our spirit: "What are my desires, my wishes, my wants, and dreams?"

If you don't look at each of these three aspects—soul, spirit, and the externalities—then you're ignoring not only the potential for transformation, but also falling prey to the belief system that human beings and the human experience is not inherently messy. You will fail to have the life you want.

You have to approach transformation in your life being willing to lose everything, willing to change everything, willing to have everything be messy. It's the fear of messiness that drives us to these simplistic, singular, one-dimensional approaches to transformation.

I had a healer tell me years ago that I had to get messy. "Get in the mud," she said. I looked at her in horror, wished I could punch her in the face (this was long before I knew how to box), and wanted to run out of there. To this day I still want to deny the mud of life. I see it in me when I look at the complexity of life in those around me and feel fix-its and judgements come up—all ways to make things more clear, clean, efficient—and less messy. I want to organize and package it and throw out all the useless crap in spring-cleaning fashion year-round. Geez. Hear my resistance to see the rich permaculture of life? I'd rather have a manicured lawn... of delusion, which takes a lot of energy to mow and maintain.

As Kabat-Zinn writes in his book *Wherever You Go, There You Are*, "You might be tempted to avoid the messiness of daily living for the tranquility of stillness and peacefulness. This, of course, would be an attachment to stillness, and like any strong attachment, it leads to delusion. It arrests development and short-circuits the cultivation of wisdom."

When we find ourselves in these patterns, we are also excluding parts of ourselves that need to be included for our wholeness. When it comes to all the parts of ourselves and psyche, we can't spring-clean them out entirely. We escape situations and in turn escape parts of ourselves that got us there in the first place. But we can't drop parts of us like lizards can drop their tails to flee a predator when in distress. We pack it all with us onto the plane, into the next gig, wherever we end up.

And there, we look at it.

WARRIOR STANCE

Real courage is risking something that might force you to rethink your thoughts and suffer change and stretch consciousness. Real courage is risking one's clichés.

—Tom Robbins

There's this thing that happens at least once during Reboot boot-camps where Jerry asks someone to stand up, feet rooted hip distance apart, arms open, palms open facing outward at waist level. We call it the warrior stance: a place to feel your rootedness and strength supporting you through the ground and at the same time feeling your vulnerable front body. It's quite the contrary stance that most entrepreneurs find themselves in, especially when they'd much rather curl up in fetal position and hide under a piano.

In the warrior stance, you can feel your front and back holding you upright and together. In an integrated way, these two parts of you are mutually supporting each other, saying "I got you" to yourself.

The strong-back, open-heart stance is the essence of leadership, especially for businesses. A strong back means support, integrity, sustainability, and fiscal responsibility. Open heart means leading authentically, moving from purpose, being vulnerable, and feeling our way through the creative edges. In building a sustainable company you need both sides. Good leaders embody paradoxical elements daily.

So, what does this warrior stance look like in action?

It looks like the moment when you move beyond the fears looming large in the theater of your own mind. It looks like saying what you need to say, even though you're convinced that once you say those words you'll be left alone, unloved and banished from the tribe (or they'll know you're an imposter, they'll take your funding away, and all your employees will leave). It looks like breaking through the delusion that as leaders at the top of chain of command we have all the answers—and admitting we need help with issues big and small that we don't have the answers to. It means taking off our game face and letting someone know how we really feel and what's really up.

The times we shift from pre-warrior to warrior are moments when, in our minds, we take a risk to voice our truth against all of our fears telling us not to. We risk in those moments what feels like an impending surefire failure. What happens instead is quite the opposite: we find ourselves in a defining moment in which we discover a new way forward, subsequently unlocking our real potential as leaders.

In the past, I've harnessed this courage with my significant other. As I stepped from pre-warrior to warrior stance, I thought I was going to say something that would certainly end our relationship. But I stayed with the words that had been brewing in my heart for the past few years and ushered them forth, clearly and articulately (and, let's be honest, through tears). My partner listened and heard me, even though it wasn't easy to hear. It made our bond stronger and we credited those conversations as the moments that took our relationship to another level.

Warrior moments break the ice that traps us. They let new life and experience flow in. The warrior stance is a way to hold yourself in life. I've often found that the conversations that scare me usually end up happening through some kismet. In those moments, I'm often surprised and relieved at what transpires. Although it was the opportunity that presented itself, it was me stepping fully into my authentic truth and connecting deep with my inner knowing—regardless of how shaky it felt to usher it forth—that made all the difference.

Holding the warrior stance as your metaphorical stance in life does more than move you beyond your fears. It allows you to come forth and be met by life. By doing so and being open to failure, you take responsibility for the direction of your life, and choose to not be reined in by fears and survival strategies from childhood. Only then can you succeed. When you dance with life from that place, without armor, you are able to be what you are, fearlessly. Being able to be quite fearlessly yourself is what it means to be a warrior.

NO GOING BACK

Back when Jerry's *Reboot* book came out, someone on our team suggested that with so much musical talent in the room we could start a company band. We could call ourselves Radical and the Inquiries, and travel as part of Jerry's book tour. Everyone found their place by volunteering instruments and skill sets—from guitars, piano, and vocals, to managing ticket sales and the schwag booth. Someone suggested that we revise Johnny Paycheck's song from "Take This Job and Shove It" to "Take This Job and Love It." After all, that very shift in tunes comprises so much of the revised lyricism that we help our clients write for themselves.

Folks come to us at various stages of burnout, moments of transition and trial, or when they know what got them here won't get them where they need and want to go. For most, this is an inflection point that denotes a pending change away from what came before, even though what comes next might be unclear. The choice is to opt for something better, something more suitable and sustainable, and that may feel entirely new at the edge of what's possible.

What leads us to burnout is not an essential factor in success, and clearly not an essential factor in achieving successful well-being for anyone. Yet we don't always believe that having what we want (and what's good for our well-being) is possible at the intersections of work and life and purpose. Our well-being, however, is necessary to doing good work. And good work is necessary for our well-being. Being attuned to our well-being is vital for taking the lead role in our life.

We often hear doubts and disbeliefs mumbling from clients in a conundrum: Can I really have the life that supports me, and do good work? Is it really "work" if I'm not stressed and panting all the time? Building something and maintaining well-being is not about "not working hard," but we can certainly work smartly to orient ourselves differently in our approach to work.

Working in accordance with our well-being is an important threshold to cross, especially when it comes to our relationship to work. If we are in control of our own lives in the choices we make, we can blaze our trails with all that fosters well-being. You can choose *you* versus choosing to sacrifice or compromise you for someone else, an ethos, or vision. The questions to ask are: Who am I, and what do I need to be fully me? Where do I collapse my boundaries and lose myself?

One aspect of any healthy relationship, including a work one, is knowing who you are and where you are in space as a complete being. Then you can be in relation to others who are also whole and complete in their space. Through this space between, there is room for connection and mutual respect of our differentiated selves. Think of two circles side by side, but not overlapping. These circles are not consuming each other. They stand together, equal, each as whole parts in communion.

To stand in your circle means to feel yourself, differentiated. Sometimes, the fear we can feel in the mumbling conundrum about having well-being and doing good work is the fear of being consumed (again, OMG, ugh!) by something. How could it be so good when it always seems to end up so badly? Such a situation is a legit uncomfortable and diminishing place to be. Yet so often we forget that as adults the powers vested in us allow us to make better choices, and not be subsumed by the younger reasoning that has lodged into our shrinking or other self-denying patterning.

Ultimately, the choice at this crux is, Do I choose myself?

When you choose yourself, you do not abandon yourself. Your well-being is the greatest act of love. It's the greatest gift you can give others and the world. Radical self-care is a revolutionary act in that if you are being true to yourself, you're anchored from an inner locus, and rooted in a way that defies any subscription to lemming mentality or what you think you *should* do. You're not leading from an outer locus, hooked on the externalities and wishes and wants of what the outside world asks of you and your attention. You're not a passenger on someone else's ship. No, you're the captain of your own.

Leading from this place could be called leading from love. It could be called "letting the soft animal of your body love what it loves" (à la poet Mary Oliver). You're leading from an inner knowing, guided by what you need for your well-being, and your choices hinge on integrity to that. Your connection to the world—to work, to lovers, to partners, to family—hinge on integrity to that. That could be the hardest work we do *before*, *as*, and *when* we commit to focusing on companies we'd be proud to work for.

From there, there's no going back to burnout-land. You've taken refuge and sanctuary in your very self. This is the BIG move. This becomes your ground. This is how you protect your magic. This is how you become a good lover—of yourself, and others—so that the world is filled with better leaders. This is how you begin to write your version of "Take This Job and Love It."

Burnt Out and Depleted

The way our world rewards success often requires splitting off what we're feeling on the inside, putting on a public face, and powering through. What we present as polished and professional covers our stress, fears, griefs, exhaustion, and longings. Ultimately, we often ignore our body and its signals to keep on going. What we push aside on our insides in order to be productive, efficient worker bees eventually catches up with us in the form of poor mental health states and burnout. Someone wins in this game, but it's not always us. However, we do get to weigh in on whether the cost incurred for the success we stand to gain is worth the drain and depletion. Ask yourself the following:

> - What depletes you?
> - Where and when do you cave in?
> - What parts of yourself do you lose?
> - When you've reached burnout in the past, what brought you back to life?
> - How can you take a stand on your own two feet and relate from that place?

THE COMPULSION TO WORK: DO YOU WORK TOO MUCH?

Ever found yourself on a free weekend afternoon reaching for your phone or laptop to get a few work-related things done? What is it that makes you choose to work during a free block of time on a weekend? Are you the type who is smart enough to break for the gym and food, but thinks about work over dinner or through a date night and then hops back on your device for a few more hours before bed? What is that impulse?

The compulsion to work arises out of a variety of fears and drivers. Some of us get dopamine hits for our outputs and associate productivity for meaning—without it, we feel empty. Others are afraid to slow down or stop for fear of becoming irrelevant. Still more are driven by perfectionism or chased to work by other powerful demons such as shame. And some of us are under the spell of hustle culture.

What drives you to work the way you do? Consider these prompts to uncover unconscious motivators that may be influencing your working style:

> What fuels your relationship with work?

> If you're not working, what happens for you?

> What does your organization or workplace culture say about work-life balance? How do others at the office behave regarding work-life balance?

> What are the unspoken office rules about how you are expected to work?

> What is your relationship to your work hours? What makes you stick to what's required of you? What keeps you going past "a good day's worth of work?"

> When you stay longer, start earlier, and put in more time, how does that make you feel?

> What do you know about how you show up at your best, when you are able to function most effectively?

THE OTHER SIDE OF FEAR

Fear is an old word that derives from the same roots that give us "fare," s in "thoroughfare." Although it often causes people to run away from troubling situations, at a deeper level, fear means "to go through it." The hidden purpose of fear involves bringing us closer to natural instincts for survival, but also for awakening inner resources and sharpening our intelligence when faced with true danger and the basic need to change.

—Michael Meade

Our tenacity gets us where we need to go when we have a big thing to do—something we know is right, and hard, and worth it. It gets us past the edges that threaten to stop us from moving through those new experiences with an openness and curiosity that leads us to the other side of fear, where we find ourselves and all that we've got.

In my undergraduate days back at Montana State University, I had a quote scrawled on a large index card taped to my bedroom door, which said in Sharpie: Run Towards the Volcano. It was a line from one of my horoscopes that stuck with me. The message was to move towards the thing that scares you. This became a bit of a mantra for my then twenty-something-year-old-self as I began to do new things and push the edges of my comfort zone. But mostly, it was a reminder to not retreat from my fears. (Unless, of course, it was a grizzly bear. I was in the woods—in Montana—after all.)

I began to notice *what* scared me and *how* it scared me. Then I'd learn to decipher how best to pay attention to that fear. I lived by the motto: If it scares you, you should probably do it. And that motto applied to many things—from gnarly outdoor adventures to a year of learning tango, from taking an improv course to using my voice when I had something to say. (The "saying the things" was always the hardest edge to lean into for me. It still is.)

Running towards the volcano became my inspirational image for leaning into the fears that made me want to stop and retreat. When I ran in that direction, I discovered what was on the other side of fear: I found more of me.

Each time I leaned into the vulnerable feeling at the edge of fear (once I got past the impulse to sit on a couch, kvetch to my roommates, and eat carbs to self-soothe the stress of thinking of being vulnerable), I crossed the threshold of added capacity. Each edge was the border between the known and the unknown. I willingly ventured into terra incognita with everything I had: a cute pair of shoes and some well-learned tools in my toolbelt (not all of which I needed, but there just in case). Each time I stood in the vulnerability of not knowing where I was, or what I was doing, or what was next, I met more of me as more of me showed up. In the process, I always surprised myself.

It's as if in crossing the threshold, I grew. I gained added capacity and confidence and was less afraid of things. This strength felt like a new muscle that supported me each new day and with each new encounter with life. I was moving out of fear by way of curiosity, and getting the neurochemical reward along with satisfaction, pride, and gratitude to be alive. And in the process, added some myelination to my growing confidence in myself. As I found more and more of myself, I could recognize the firmness of what that felt like, even when things felt groundless. I had the solid ground of my very self as my foundation to stand on.

Jules Pieri, author of *How We Make Stuff Now: Turn Ideas into Products That Build Successful Businesses*, defines tenacity as identifying the fear that stops you and allowing the higher part of your brain function to work with it so you move forward anyway. As entrepreneurs and artists in the maker space, and most humans endeavoring to go after something they value or desire, tenacity is exercised daily (often, moment by moment).

Tenacity is perhaps one of the most important muscles to strengthen. When things get hard or fears fill you with clouds of self-doubt and inadequacy, you build tenacity when you keep reinvesting in your product, your team, your company, your work, your partnership, your marriage, or your life—even when part of you would rather disengage.

Bringing a dream into the world, or a product to the marketplace, has a big learning-and-living-through-it curve that calls for a hearty dose of stick-with-it-tude. I spent the early part of my post—master's degree working life helping a wide range of people bring their products and services to the world via their online platform—before the internet made doing so as easy as it is these days. For many of my artist friends, this part of the process was daunting. Creating the *thing* was where their energy sang. The hard points of bringing a new creation into the world, bound for success by connecting with the folks who most needed it, brought up new edges along the execution learning curve and a lot of feelings.

Fear can be debilitating. It can stifle creativity. It can keep us small and contained in a world that seeks our gifts, our energy, our wisdom. Consider the role fear plays in how you show up in your life with these questions:

> - Where has passion and aliveness been squelched by fear in your life?
> - What's waiting for you on the other side?

> What possibility is lying dormant in yourself, waiting to meet you there?

> Where can you find your curiosity and longing towards and within life so that you can reinvest where and when needed?

WONDERING ABOUT WONDER

*May you experience each day as a sacred gift
woven around the heart of wonder.*

—John O'Donohue

Lately I've been wondering about wonder. And recently was talking to a friend about how often we fail to turn to wonder; instead, we leverage rational answers and advice-driven thinking to ease our anxieties. With surprising simplicity, she said, "Wonder seems contrary to productivity." Yet it's the most magically productive thing we can tap into, I found myself thinking! I wonder why it's a tool we leave behind in lieu of fear-based reactions like worry and anxiety (and then get spun up in the mythmaking that spins out from them). I wonder why we're not trained to trust wonder like we trust our astute rationales and logical thoughts. What would it be like if rather than chasing after answers and definitives as fervently as we do, we chased after the results born of wonder?

I keep thinking about the notion that courage is a choice and fear is a reaction. How do we lean in and harness our courageous self, especially when fear and its quick old patterns take hold? What gets us out of fear and into curiosity so that we can choose courage in the first place? I'd wager that wonder has something to do with it.

Founded in 1997 by Parker Palmer, Marcy Jackson, and Rick Jackson, the Center for Courage and Renewal has a guiding set of thirteen touchstones that inform how we can relate to each other with integrity and trust in our organizations, communities, and homes. Reboot brings these touchstones into our group experiences, like our bootcamps and circles, as guidelines to create safe spaces. We emphasize a few of them to shift the productive, problem-solving entrepreneurs in the room from jumping into fix-it mode for a different reaction entirely. These are the instructions we give them:

> When the going gets rough, turn to wonder. Turn from reaction and judgement to wonder and compassionate inquiry. Ask yourself, "I wonder why they feel/think this way?" or "I wonder what my reaction teaches me about myself?" Set aside judgement to listen to others—and to yourself—more deeply.

Wonder creates space for more transformative work to happen. The silence and lack of answers in that space can feel like the cloud of unknowing, but the great mystics knew that space well. That was the space where the world seemed to open up with insights from the inside out.

Turning to wonder is not too esoteric a concept to bring to work. It's a tool that brings us back to what's here now, even if that's a lot of things we don't want to lean into at first glance and even if we think we know the answer already. Wonder asks us to suspend what we think we know about what will or will not happen and why that is so. It reminds us that there's a lot we don't know about, and it begs us to get curious and dwell in possibility. From there, something shifts. Important conversations emerge. New insights are gleaned. We listen deeper to something beneath the words and feelings. People feel heard. We hold our presence for ourselves and one another.

Putting this into practice, how would that impact your rela-tionships at work, at home, in the world? The riddling anxiety that can arise when listening to another, or listening to our own thoughts and sorting through those feelings, makes us want an immediate response to quell all those feels. This isn't the best mode for communication at work, at home, in life—or in the ongoing inner conversation in our hearts. What happens when we jump into a fix-advise-rationalize mode with our partners, colleagues, and ourselves? We often shut down or defend against what's happening, what we're feeling—against life itself.

In so doing, we are not present. We're defending against the reality of what's happening, contracted around it. We're afraid to meet life as it's showing up.

Living and leading with integrity means listening to our own voices. It means we can stand in the swirl of our experience (feelings, thoughts, sensations, longings), even if it feels like a space without words, and be present for what unfolds without controlling what's next. From there, we can discover what's in store in that swirl of our own humanity. If we can do that for ourselves, we stand a greater chance of being able to hold space for others when they are in their own swirl-of-humanity moment.

Such a stance is life-giving. Perhaps as a mark of resiliency, when the going gets tough, the tough turn to wonder. Like curiosity, wonder feels expansive in our bodies, whereas fear feels like a contraction. It's a response to life akin to opening all the windows to let in air versus locking all the doors and battening the hatches. It allows us to find our way in the labyrinth of our own experience by living it rather than curling up in the fetal position to merely get through it. Wonder is that place where we suspend our defenses, our judgements, our fears, and open to the possibility of what else might be here, now, and get curious about it.

Turning to wonder moves you to stand with the courage to open up to other possibilities and double-click into your experience to see what else is there beyond the anxieties, old-stories, knee-jerk pseudo-sage placating advice giving. It allows you the presence to ask these important questions:

> What's important here?

> What's arising that is calling for more of my attention?

> What's asking me to look and listen more closely with the eyes and ears of the heart?

> What's coming up for me that I need to look at more closely as I listen to someone else's story?

With wonder at the helm, you can sit at the edge of what you don't know and feel into what you do. You stand a chance at staying present, keeping fear and its wired reactions at bay. You stand a chance at doing something new, therefore allowing something different to happen. If we make a conscious effort to be with ourselves and others in this way, what impact might that have?

GENTLE STRENGTH

"What does courage mean?" asked the boy.
"To tell the truth of who you are with your
whole heart," said the horse.

—Charlie Mackesy

How many of us had moments in our very young lives when we were hurt by some circumstance, and then created coping armor as our self-preservation senses took hold to keep us safe? Unfortunately, even though that hardened callus of strength formed to try and protect us in the past, it can end up disregarding the very parts of us it's trying to shield from danger.

For me, this tough skin has meant being cautious to share what really matters to me, rarely asking for help or support, not fully trusting others will deliver or keep their word, and being poised to be disappointed by what they do deliver (only then to do it myself anyway).

Needless to say, it's been hard to trust anyone but me *with* me throughout my life. So I keep a lot locked down behind a pleasant smile, a veneer of *fine*, a highly-refined blend of wit and humor that my partner refers to as a "can of snark," and a seemingly misanthropic behavior set. It's my go-to out in the world.

Wrapped inside of that tart candy-coated shell is a whole lot of things: big ideas and desires, longings, and gobs of feelings about myself, life, work, my people, worries, questions, and uncertainties. There's a lot of Big Love things (the stuff that makes me feel expansive), and a lot of fears (the stuff that makes me feel less than expansive). Mostly, there's a whole lot of human truth in my internal status, yet much of it feels too tender to share, too tender to trust that it will be held by an equally tender heart on the receiving end.

Somewhere in my history as a little person, perhaps I needed things and the folks in charge didn't deliver. Or perhaps the sensitive and important things weren't met with the same gravitas by others as I felt in my little heart. The way we cope and manage our deep and early hurts shapes how we roll through life: where we're guarded, and what we're open about. For some, it's a chip on the shoulder, a wall of armor, weaponized sarcasm, or a highly philosophical stance that denies emotions and spirituality, and treats folks as if they are software (even Brené Brown, in *Braving the Wilderness*, notes how her young life, fraught with parental issues, made her forego all emotions for data). We each have our own way of keeping our most true and tender spots behind locked doors, which can lead us to fail to ask for or receive help, voice our needs, or say the things most important to us—all in an attempt to protect ourselves.

We stay tight like a fist to tough it out, wholly independent as we are and so proud of it. But that stance is often lonely, and it leaves us closed off from the potential healing the world has to offer.

Self-preservation is a genius mechanism. However, operating out of toughness isn't always the best modus operandi, nor is it the bravest. Resiliency does not mean building a wall to protect you from life. As you seal off the hurts or guard potential hurts by closing yourself off, you lose your full range of movement as if guarding a physical injury. Operating to keep pain at bay can confine us to a limited set of experiences and ways of relating to others and ourselves. Being a tough cookie can only get you so far, and it can keep you distant from what you really want.

That message we so often hear—*toughen up!*—offers a false sense of strength when we're being challenged by what haunts us, or when we want to be freely ourselves in the world. The strength we're looking for isn't a tough shell, but rather an unshakeable inner resolve that shows up with compassion for ourselves. Though a gentler stance, it's by no means weak. Strength comes from knowing who you are, what your boundaries are, and that you are the only one who can really reject you. Strength by any other name is just a posturing of defenses.

Being vulnerable, voicing needs and desires, asking for what you want, voicing your truth, and sharing the big ideas most important to you are moments that require you to show up with the courage to have your heart broken.

A certain grace can find you in those moments of vulnerability and gentleness, when you realize your shell of defenses can be shed for a slightly more permeable space. Where your inner life meets the world, and the world meets you back, is where the magic happens. We can expand in that space and not let our fears keep us small. Being vulnerable together requires an act of love.

Part IV

EMBRACING CHANGE

FRESH TRACKS

Growing up in West Central Wisconsin, I know intimately the inhospitable season that is winter—the kind that will drive you crazy until you learn to get out into it. That's what I learned to do way back in my high school years: I ventured out in a pair of snowshoes to ward off the restlessness of cabin fever.

There were no groomed trails out near the county line where we lived, so I blazed my own through the neighboring woods, along the creeks and to the edge of the Chippewa River. The light of the warm house glowed in the distance as I walked through the insular crystalline blanket on the earth. It was quiet. Still. I could hear nothing but the sound of falling snow, the shush of the snowshoes through the powder, and my heartbeat pulsing loudly.

I set out because I needed a shift, a change of space—a new experience and way to be in this winter. I had a rough knowledge of the landscape in the area but had never traveled these paths before. I trusted my homing pigeon instinct to get me home at winter light's curfew. As pedestrian as it was, these expeditions were exhilarating. While adventuring out, I found I was going in. Those lines in the snow became a whole new form of journaling.

Parker Palmer, in his book *Let Your Life Speak*, applies the same "get out into it" advice to our inner winters, which may take many forms: failure, betrayal, depression, among them. He writes: "Until we enter boldly into the fears we most want to avoid, those fears will dominate our lives. But when we walk directly into them, protected from frostbite by the warm garb of friendship or inner discipline or spiritual guidance—we can learn what they have to teach us."

This adventuring inward takes courage. Facing fears takes courage. Change takes courage. A dear mentor once told me that our habitual patterns of being are neurologically much like the well-worn rut of a sledding path that's been used over and over again. In order to change, we need to pick up the sled and move it to a patch of fresh powder and open up a wholly new, potentially exhilarating experience. In these moments of awareness and choice in the process of change, I am reminded of Thich Nhat Hanh's gentle reminder of how to proceed: "Breath. Smile. Go slowly." That quality of pace tempers any fear that may arise as one ventures out into something new.

I find something enticing about the sound of stepping out into freshly fallen snow. Every day, I decide to make fresh tracks in my way of being in my own life. I hope that you also find opportunities to be met with a stillness that reminds you softly, profoundly, that every day is a journey, and the journey itself is home.

UNFINISHED POEMS

I would love to live
Like a river flows,
Carried by the surprise
Of its own unfolding.

—John O'Donohue

"It takes a lot to trust what's emerging in any given moment," meditation teacher and entrepreneur Vince Horn once said to me. We'd been talking about leading from the heart, the balance of being and doing, and the delicate balance between forcing something to fruition or holding the process with the space of allowing.

I'm not a huge fan of surprises. I love me a plan. I love to-do lists, checklists, and the itemized steps to get 'er done with ease and flow. While the one thing I can always seem to count on is change, I tend to forget that part. When things go awry, it can set off an array of feelings and thoughts in me that I hadn't planned on. But there they are, whether I like them or not. I mutter a facetious curse to impermanence and, hopefully, laugh. (Impermanence is both the bane and boon of my existence.)

In those moments, I don't always know when to push to make something happen or when to be still, to give it time, to trust that the universe is unfolding as it should. Something happens on that bridge between analytical and introspective. I feel into what's happening for me in that moment:

> What's my fear?

> What's the root of my anxiety?

> What does this situation really need?

> Is my first reaction a gut feeling to act upon, or am I coming from a place of wanting to take care of or control something so I can ease my not knowing, my anxiety, my unsettled feelings?

When leading with an open heart, our fear isn't trying to control the spontaneous co-arisings of life happening before us. We're able to meet whatever's right in front of us with an agile "this-is-so, so-what" stance. Yet there are many ways we try to contain things: asserting our solutions and fixes onto others, analysis paralysis, burying ourselves in the myth of our busyness, to name a few.

In his book *Pronoia*, Rob Brezsny created a list of actions most likely to wound the soul, which he calls the Four Foolish Virtues. I wonder if any of these feel familiar to you:

1. Being analytical to such extremes that you repress your intuition

2. Sacrificing your pleasure through a compulsive attachment to duty

3. Tolerating excessive stress because you assume it helps you accomplish more

4. Being so knowledgeable that you neglect your curiosity

I'd be remiss not to mention that I see all four of his points as the root of what drives folks in the tech/startup industry to depression and burnout. I encourage you to sit with them for a while.

The more I try to control life, the more I find myself let down by the illusion of control and cut off from life itself. Because what's lost when I try to contain everything is a rich connection to that life which is emerging within and around me.

When I'm able to see that I'm being held and part of something greater, it's easier for me to trust what's emerging. I trust my intuition. I find that I'm less hasty to make decisions. I breathe deeper. I'm less reactive to the need for an immediate response. I'm less frenetic in my work, not anxious about what I have to do. I'm more present in conversations. I ask better questions. I let life in close, and closer still.

Brené Brown has a passage on intuition—and why we avoid it—in her book *The Gifts of Imperfection*. She's found that what silences our intuitive voice is our need for certainty. "Most of us are not very good at not knowing," she writes. "We like sure things and guarantees so much that we don't pay attention to the outcomes of our brain's matching process." You know those times when you ignore a strong internal instinct; instead you become fearful and look for assurance from others, asking What do you think? Should I do it? What would you do? That's exactly what she's talking about.

Brown goes on to explain another example of how our need for certainty sabotages our intuition in those moments "when we ignore our gut's warning to slow down, gather more information, or reality-check our expectations." This happens when we say to ourselves things like:

I'm just going to do it. I don't care anymore.
I'm tired of thinking about it. It's too stressful.
I'd rather just do it than wait another second.
I can't stand not knowing.

Ultimately, she defines intuition this way: "Intuition is not a single way of knowing—it's our ability to hold space for uncertainty and our willingness to trust the many ways we've developed knowledge and insight, including instinct, experience, faith, reason." Intuition allows us to wait in the vulnerable space of not knowing and allow for things to emerge to help us decide mindfully what we need to do.

Intuition is a willingness to be surprised and surrender our need to control the uncomfortable feelings of uncertainty and fear. If we can bring this to bear in our lives, we live like unfinished poems, feeling into the next line, even if it's a long pause, welcoming the surprise of our own unfolding.

THE BEAUTY OF NOT KNOWING

When I was running operations at a company years ago, I brought in this piece of fortune cookie wisdom from my art studio and taped it to my monitor: "Creativity requires the courage to let go of certainties." With everything seemingly changing or shifting daily, that little note seemed to capture the nature of my role at the time in which not everything went according to plan, systems had to change, and I felt like I was flying by the seat of my pants.

Most of the time, I was creating something new. I met many of my edges and iterated beyond them. There were days I had no idea what I was doing. There were days that I had a clue. There were days I had to scrap what I did yesterday because things had changed again. Change was the one constant. While I knew this was all part of the process, it could be disorienting and messed with my penchant for planning.

What I learned in that role felt like the MBA I didn't know I wanted or needed. And the more I learned, the more I knew what I didn't know, as if my surface area with uncertainty was expanding in proportion to any newly gleaned information and experience. What I brought to that role was the knowledge of how to orient myself in the midst of all the questions and who-knows-what-else that was just around the corner ready to present itself. I likened it to a big art project. Every day was just another day in the studio.

Life changes constantly. That means uncertainty and fear, and even more possibility and movement.

Our human wiring and programming can sometimes make it hard to endure that change without struggle. But our capacity for greater personal resiliency also makes it possible for us to seize those moments ripe with endless possibility and unknowns. In times when fear makes us cower into a stream of thoughts that articulate what we know we *don't* want to have happen, what we fear, or what we're worried about, there's always an unlimited number of things that *could* go in our favor in that same moment. When the unknowns arise to stop us in our tracks, we can turn towards what's in front of us and see what else it holds—if we can pause the impending thoughts of doom long enough. It helps to turn to wonder then and ask ourselves: Hmmm, wouldn't it be great if… (e.g., something better, something I hadn't thought of or planned for yet, happened instead?)

And wouldn't it be great if those moments we'd oft dubbed *failures* were instead seen as changes that moved us in a better direction that we didn't know we needed or wanted? We'd then begin celebrating those moments as wake-up calls that can usher in more of what we'd really like into our life. Musing on the possibilities provides a shift out of the swirling vortex of anxiety, and offers a better deal: an open stance that has space and allows for something new to meet you.

It's a moment of creative agency. We may not always know what we're doing but we can feel our way through, living into all the unanswered questions. Pausing long enough on the crux between a fear response and opening to something new, we can suss out our next bold move, even if that move is no movement at all. The beauty lies in recognizing that we, too, are in process.

In this way, as the artist, you are the work. I'd render that to say you're an entire body of work. Success here is defined in terms of your becoming from moment to moment. And work becomes a means to become more human, more fully you.

Embracing this means that our body of work takes a lifetime of enduring creativity (or creative enduring)—whether we are consciously working at our process or not. We let go of certainties except for what is present for us. Edward Abbey once wrote about photography that "our job is to record, each in his own way, this world of light and shadow and time that will never come again exactly as it is today." I'd say this applies to life as a whole. Each in our own way, in our own process of becoming, every moment is itself only a snapshot of a larger transition into which we know not quite what.

If we cling to those moments as if they are still photographs, we risk being caught up in the nets of attachment that stagnate or eddy our progress. Yet we can begin to trust what's moving us into the unlimited possibility at the horizon line and beyond. That's quite an edge—moving into constant newness and allowing it to happen with a sense of sweet surrender. All we know for sure is what's in front of us and what we sense within us. So often we want to revert to what we've done before, what we know as tried and true, rather than open up to the larger mystery.

In his book *The Poetics of Space*, philosopher Gaston Bachelard explains that "we cover the universe with drawings we have lived. These drawings need not be exact. They need only to be tonalized on the mode of our inner space."

I am reminded of what artist Roderick MacIver wrote in *Art as a Way of Life*:

> The ancient roots of the word "art" have to do with connection, and art, at its best, is our connection to the mystery, to the parts of ourselves that are deeper and truer than the day-to-day world. Art connects us to our dreams, to the things that can't be explained in words, to the things that

have touched our core, to our imaginary worlds, and even to our own personal chaos. Art has something to do with the part that doesn't want to be tamed, that can't be tamed. Our challenge as artists is to muster the technique, the vision, the persistence, and emotional courage to explore what means most to us. Our challenge as people is even greater—to live a life that is in itself is a work of art.

By owning that we as humans are in the process of becoming, we therefore are also accepting our inherent wholeness. The drawings we have lived shape us as much as we shape them. Our lives are our body of work. So you may not know what you are doing, but you know you, and that creative exploration is your greatest work.

PASSING BY

In one of my first creative journals, I captured this quote by photographer Henri Cartier-Bresson: "What is real is the continual change of form: form is only a snapshot view of transition."

These words were written sideways on a page spread next to these notes:

> The point is to learn to remember that we might have been otherwise, and might yet be. —Donna J. Haraway

> Nevertheless, the illusion of self–created by our memories, mental conditioning, and sensory inability to detect our body's constant state of change–helps give us the impression that we are "always" the same person. In fact, ... we die and are reborn from instant to instant to instant. —Jack Maguire, *Essential Buddhism*, p. 101

And then I found this fragment from the Diamond Sutra of Mahāyāna Buddhism, which is often read at memorial services:

> Thus shall you think of all this fleeting world:
> A star at dawn, a bubble in a stream;
> A flash of lightning in a summer cloud,
> A flickering lamp, a phantom, a dream.

At first glance, it's all about transitoriness. But somewhere close, sifting through that mix of notes on those pages, was a celebration of spontaneity. It was tucked in there, next to the human desire to map things and hold tight to the map, despite the fact that "the map is not the territory."*

Sometimes I forget that this—this moment, this feeling, this body—is all temporary. Every moment is a snapshot of a larger transition underway, an arc with a trajectory I'm not entirely privy to. I often forget that I am fluid and in flux, in a perpetual process of becoming. I consider myself to be a fixed and separate identity at times—one of the three tragic misunderstandings that creates dissatisfaction and suffering within life, as Pema Chödrön notes in *Comfortable with Uncertainty*. The other two are expecting that change should be graspable and predictable, and reaching for something else to ease the edginess of the moment (otherwise known as looking for happiness in all the wrong places), each of which escalates our dissatisfaction.

This wish to make life permanent and predictable is a sticky place for us humans, who are constantly in process. The wish to control uncertainty is really a denial of life as it is right now. Life doesn't happen in frozen moments. Yet we continually go back to the things we've frozen in time; we pine for them, cling to them, and deny what's happening right in front of our nose—and this creates suffering. As Chödrön notes, "We spend all our energy and waste our lives trying to re-create these zones of safety, which are always falling apart."

Those zones of safety can sometimes be our exterior lives built to protect a sense of solid identity—or an external shell of it. Yet the perfect life on paper (or on the internet) is not always aligned with the interior landscape of our inner life. The inner happenings can be radically disparate from the glossy façades projected outward.

---

* This phrase, coined by the Polish American philosopher and engineer Alfred Korzybski, is meant to describe the difference between actual reality (the territory) and our perception of it (the map).

That incongruity can cause great pain; it's a quandary for being authentic. Parker Palmer refers to this as "the divided life."

Elisabeth Kübler-Ross, a Swiss American psychiatrist who authored the groundbreaking work *On Death and Dying*, wrote, "We run after values that, at death, become zero. At the end of your life, nobody asks you how many degrees you have, or how many mansions you built, or how many Rolls Royces you could afford. That's what dying patients teach you." Façades aren't generative things to live for, but the vitality flowing through you is. When both inner and outer align, the values that you live for amount to a much richer life.

One of the exercises we sometimes use at bootcamp asks participants to write their own eulogies. It's like a pre-mortem to expose one's inner and outer incongruencies. More often than not, it leads to dramatic reprioritizing and a truing up of one's inner life and outer experiences.

Remember, this is your one wild and precious life. And as Mary Oliver asks of us, what will you do with it? Begin to explore that deep question by asking yourself:

> What do you love about what you do?
> What does life have in store for you that you may be shutting out?
> What are you missing out on by clinging to external values that are unaligned with your deepest longings?
> What transitions do you want or need to make?
> What do you need to leave behind? What is ready to die? What old skins might you need to shed?
> What is emerging for you?

In a world where all is temporary, consider what choices are you making: in your leadership, in your work, and in your life.

WHEN LIFE COMES AT YOU

When we try to protect ourselves from the inevitability of change,
we are not listening to the soul. We are listening to our fear of
life and death, our lack of faith, our smaller ego's will to prevail.
To listen to your soul is to stop fighting with life—to stop fighting
when things fall apart; when they don't go our way, when we get
sick, when we are betrayed or mistreated or misunderstood. To
listen to the soul is to slow down, to feel deeply, to see ourselves
clearly, to surrender to discomfort and uncertainty and to wait.

—Elizabeth Lesser

I'm often amazed at how I think I can control the interdependent co-arising* of life. With all the phenomena unfurling and folding around me, there's an infinite number of things happening outside the realm of my control.

The good and beautiful surprises don't get to me so much as the other side of impermanence: the people, places, and things that aren't going my way, are not what I want to be, are making me upregulated or feel helpless. The latter pile of happenings—all those things I can't control—usually make me entirely anxious. Which then pushes me to want a plan to manage everything, or, even better, clean something. Most of the time I do both.

---

* This is a central Buddhist concept that everything in existence—including thoughts, feelings, lives, objects, and systems—arises as a result of, and is dependent on, other things. That is, everything is connected.

I know it's delusional to think that cleaning my house does anything to control the entropic chaos out in the world just beyond my doorstep. I have a hard time with the random and unpredictable nature of life, which I try hard to offset in a myriad of ways that I actually think I influence.

It's unsettling to think that no matter how many fresh-pressed juices, freeze-dried superfood powders, grass-fed Level 4 meats, and bone broth with organic ghee I consume along with my doctor-recommended supplements, I still end up with a chronic illness that takes years to heal. It doesn't make sense and it doesn't seem fair. Following steps A, B, and C doesn't mean that I've spared myself from the suffering I was intending to ward off with a gluten-sugar-dairy-caffeine-grain-and-fun-free life addicted to purity. Even in my attempts to consume beyond medical reproach and embody the pinnacle of health, there is so much out of my control and awareness that I don't really stand a chance at attaining that goal.

I have only a modicum of control over what happens to me. I have only my choices and my actions. That's all I got in the massive control panel as a human. Two buttons. Infinite possibilities. Though when I start fearing life coming at me, the modes of control I tend to employ are usually isolating and limiting. Before you know it, I will resign myself to never leaving the house.

"The world is a terrifying place. We manage it by believing we can control it. And when it hasn't been controlled—when it doesn't bend to our wills—we either look for something to blame, or we surrender," wrote Heather Kirn Lanier in her epic essay "Superbabies Don't Cry."

The fullness of life includes suffering, the thing we want most to keep at bay. Suffering, and all the feels therein, is part of what this life is about.

When we can surrender to that fact, away from convenient comfort and security, we find freedom in those uncertain, maybe even shaky terrains. Being in the unmapped space feels alive at that point where fear shifts to excitement within us. And we have an inner confidence, an "I got this" stance about us, that lets us meet life on its terms without wanting to shoot the messenger.

Our body gives us no shortage of signs that we're stressed by the perceived terrors of life. We restrict in the fighting, a bracing against our own failure to accept what life is coming at us. Our anxiety is a sign that we're stuck in that current. And then we'll exercise our favorite defenses and fear-of-life coping tactics. These motifs can get especially gnarly when it comes to relating with people.

But these moments of anxiety are opportunities to look deeper and ask yourself the following questions:

> When is anxiety is present for you?

> What does that feel like? Where does it live in your body?

> What memories, sounds or images are present for you as you feel into it?

> What is that anxiety trying to tell you?

> How old is that message?

> What are your go-to responses for managing that anxiety?

> How does that response serve you, the situation, or your relationships?

> What might help you move beyond the anxiety?

As you become more comfortable with these inquiries, you may find the courage to step into the unknown and unchartered territory of your own growth and change.

BETWIXT

I always joke that impermanence is the bane of my existence. When something in my life changes, either with or without warning, I realize I'm banking on the illusion that things will always stay the same. And when I do have to face the fact that the only constant is impermanence, it's like flying into the window of reality—really fast—and I have to buffer it with a wee bit of humor to soften the blow. When things I hang part of my heart on leave or disappear, I'm left with a gap in the life I'd known. A beloved horse dies overnight. My partner receives alarming news from the heart doctor. My favorite restaurant no longer delivers. "Dang impermanence," I'll mutter, only partially in jest. It's hard to cover up the loss, hurt, sadness, grief, anger that's not too far below the surface.

I don't like all the feels that arise when the plot shifts. As much as I may secretly fancy myself a trendsetter, I have mixed feelings about change. That's really it: change produces a custom blend of excitement and fear, shaken up with a lot of *what's next?* questions, that pours over my nervous system. "Oh shoot," I think. "What am I going to do now?" It's easy to feel groundless when some of the knowns that have anchored your paths, that you've devoted your attention to, are threatened or no longer there.

A life lived is certainly a page-turner. There are many flavors of plot twists, some of which John O'Donohue calls "threshold moments." One minute you're living out your life, and the next you get a call that shifts things entirely: she's pregnant; they're pulling out their funding commitment; he died by suicide. To quote meditation teacher Emily Horn, "Consciousness is so turbulent." Or as my rolfer says, "Life isn't for amateurs."

When change happens, we're affected with a variety of feels in varying degrees of intensity. We move from a job, shift careers, shut down or open a new relationship or startup, feel a shift in our role as founder and suddenly find ourselves in (or on the brink of) an in-between moment. Most of the time, those moments are filled with more questions than answers. The world can feel turned upside down and we can feel shaky.

In each of the big shifts in my life, I've felt like I was shifting paradigms, shedding skins, molting into something new. Some junctures felt like reinventing myself, some felt like a metamorphosis was underway. (Metamorphosis is always a bit scary, because in that cocooned in-between time, your old self melts down caterpillar-to-butterfly style.) Leaving one state or one role or one relationship always brings me to the in-between, which is both as uncomfortable as it can be but also allows me to sense what is emerging in the larger field of my life.

We commit to the things we show up to every day. We can "eat-sleep-breathe" something for long days upon long days, year after year, and weave excitement and hopes and dreams into it that orients much of our attention. As we are in relation to our work, our partners, and our company vision, we keep signing up by showing up. We stay wound up in the stories we tell ourselves about why we're doing what we do. Through growth and expanded perspectives, we may realize that the old story isn't working and we're not growing where we are, or we realize we're not where we're supposed to be or that it won't turn out as we'd hoped. It's hard to leave when you've wrapped your hands and head and heart around something, even if you do feel the ways in which it limits you.

Maybe the role shifts, maybe you shift. Maybe you start a family and new priorities create a cascade of many shifts. Maybe the market shifts. Whatever happens, you find yourself at the end of the chapter, turning the page.

As Marilyn Ferguson writes in *The Aquarian Conspiracy: Personal and Social Transformation in Our Time*, "It's not so much that we're afraid of change or so in love with the old ways, but it's that place in between that we fear... It's like being between trapezes. It's Linus when his blanket is in the dryer. There's nothing to hold on to."

Finding yourself betwixt is a potent space of the human experience. How do we use these moments served up by our startups and our lives to grow? How can we use the in-between time to look at the operating systems we hold and determine what needs a refresh? What is there to learn about ourselves and how we do life? How can we embrace the change and shifts as opportunities to lift our head up from the ol' work piles and rabbit holes and shift our gaze up to the horizon line, to sense what's calling us? How can we rise to the call of what life is asking of us, above and beyond what we may have previously subscribed our attention to? How can we live aware of what's emerging in us?

Growing Is Not Easy: Coming Out of Your Shell

Molting isn't an easy endeavor. It's a stressful process that requires much energy and leaves the soft crustacean body without its hard shell and strong pincers, vulnerable to predators before the new exoskeleton forms. One of the tragic end-of-life risks for older lobsters is that due to the energy expenditure of molting, they can get stuck in a too-small shell and rot from the inside out.

As humans, we're lucky in the sense that our risks of failing to grow are less graphic. However different in process, they are not any tidier than what lobsters go through. The molting that happens as we grow, and the number of skins we shed throughout our lifetimes, has a similar line of vulnerability.

As you work to unburden yourself of old habits, old feelings, and old coverings that no longer help you move forward, ask yourself the following:

> What are my lobster moments? What are some big moltings I've had in my life?

> Where am I now in my exoskeleton? How does it fit? How are things feeling? Where am I growing out of my old skin? What right now might be molting for me?

> How can I be gentle with myself as I grow into more of me?

THRESHOLDS OF CHANGE

*Threshold, noun: the magnitude or intensity that
must be exceeded for a certain reaction, phenomenon,
result, or condition to occur or be manifested.*

—Oxford English Dictionary

A life that looks good on paper but leaves you feeling various forms of stressed lets you know it's time to get curious about what's up. A tension/relaxation litmus is a good barometer to heed as you make choices in your job, your career, your partnerships, your relationships, your family, and what to do for the holidays. Yet how often do we ignore that basic rubric in lieu of sticking it out with something that doesn't quite fit?

Just last weekend I ran into a friend who was contemplating a transition in her work life. She's a VP at a large healthcare provider and was sharing how she was looking at other offers on the West Coast, and horse properties in the same area. She lit up with possibility, and then her demeanor shifted. "I don't know if I should complain," she confessed, as if she was doing something wrong by considering other options. "I mean, life is pretty good right now. On paper, it's *the* life. But I'm depressed and burnt out, so something doesn't feel right." I could feel her internal struggle: if what she had was *enough* by external standards, she shouldn't kvetch or want or wonder what else might be out there.

Even if life looks good on paper, if you're depressed and burnt out, that's not much of a life, is it? What keeps us in the job that feels bad, or in the relationship that sucks the air out of us (but maybe looks good in your highlight reel)?

When the looks-good-on-paper life falls flat in the fulfillment category, paying keen attention to our longing can lead us to something more satisfying and grounding—like our own sense of aliveness. From there, we can live from an inner locus, versus the more suffocating outer locus where we try to meet the world's (or our parents') image of what to do and how to be. We need to harness our inner iconoclast to determine when enough is enough.

Growing up and becoming an adult is about learning what stories, beliefs, and strategies are running your life, and which ones you've long outgrown. What are the images of success you've been setting out for, and are those yours or someone else's? It's about finding yourself, knowing yourself intimately, and knowing in your core who you are, what you want, and when it's time to change.

Our internal thresholds can be a tricky place to navigate alone. The desire to shift current lived limitations bumps up against the world of our parents and ancestors, and the lessons they imparted upon us—consciously and unconsciously. We bump up against the external directives set by the collective *they* who project images of success, failure, and all that you can be and should be if you want to measure up. Standing in the midst of what's coming at us and what came before us, trying to figure out where to go, can pose a directional challenge on our journey to find belonging. Until we sort it all out and identify all our operating parts, all those external forces will likely weigh in on our decision making. So consider beginning your journey by asking:

> Where have shame and guilt ruled your decisions?

> How are you living out someone else's dreams for you versus your own?

> What do you do to find love, recognition, or success that sacrifices yourself and your aliveness?

As humans, we're each able to withstand unique levels of discomfort from physical, emotional, and mental stress based on the thermostat settings that have been programmed into us by learning and experience. We may repeat these situations more often than seems necessary, as if the tripped switch of our brain wiring deems these patterns inevitable. As my teacher Carl Buchheit says, "The things we've learned to survive often become the things upon which our survival depends." Remove the survival situation or stimulus and the system could break (according to the part of us that kept us alive this long). A strange trick of our neurology: it keeps us small, stuck, and cycling through limitations that don't have to define us.

Our capacity to feel joy also has an internal thermostat setting that tells us how much joy is okay for us to handle safely. The good news is that we can work with these settings to produce more of the good stuff and less of the not-so-good stuff.

When tension arises it's a signal that our proverbial stuff is coming up, and it's time to look at that. It can help us know when to decouple our well-being from the external forces competing for our lifeforce. Sometimes tension is a sign that something needs to shift in our current situation, whether workable or not. After you travel down the road of radical self-inquiry, the edges of what you want and how you feel you should be become more apparent. Perhaps then, the choice becomes clear and more attuned to *you* without the extraneous voices vying for your attention, time, energy.

This is a deeper dive into knowing who you are. A bit of excavation into the parts that make up you and make up your mind. As you venture down this path, you arrive closer to the soul, and you learn to value what your soul is offering you in this lifetime.

How do we live so we keep our souls intact? How do we let our souls flourish?

HELLO, BUTTERFLY

Just last week I was laying half-naked on my side on my rolfer's bodywork table, staring at the series of images he has on the wall while my fascia received some much-needed attention to organize my body better in gravity. The photos depicted a butterfly's metamorphosis. I've been mesmerized by these images for years. My favorite is the first in the series: a solo chrysalis attached to a twig. The enclosure looks at once calm and intense; the pressure cooker where meltdown and change is securely taking place.

Metamorphosis is the ultimate journey of transformation. It's a remarkable feat of heeding the call of something beyond yourself, enduring a process of dissolution, and emerging into a wholly new, brilliant, fluttering thing. "What the caterpillar calls the end of the world, the master calls a butterfly," wrote Chuang Tzu. What emerges is not only a wholly new being, but also a wholly different view of things and way of being in the world.

I feel like I've been there before: cocooned, turned on my head, restricted but not resisting all while my old self dissolves, becoming nutritious soup for the newly forming structure of me. In fact, I feel like I've been there numerous times before, each at a turning point in my life. Some of those turning points were matters of circumstance, others were more organic changes in direction, as if my inner compass was turning me towards the future that was mine beyond the horizon line. Each of them seemed to require an entirely new wardrobe by the end of it all.

Transformation in the human realm is a more drawn-out process than what caterpillars go through to become butterflies. It seems we have more than one chrysalis moment to hold and morph us into newer versions of ourselves. (Or as I read somewhere on the internet recently: "Every next level of your life will demand a different you.") Much like a caterpillar no longer content with inching around on the ground eating grass all day, we must heed the call for change with the courage to look within for our precious budding wings.

This kind of looking inward is far from navel gazing. It is the work that shapes and reshapes our perceptions so that we encounter and sense the world differently than before. This is not indulgent philosophical meandering along the pathways of your mental formations. It is embodied knowledge. This isn't an upleveling you can hack. À la Keats, it's about living into "the holiness of the heart's affections, and the truth of imagination." It requires a journey into the heart and trusting the mystery of what's unfolding. As Wendell Berry wrote in *The Unforeseen Wilderness*:

> And the world cannot be discovered by a journey of miles, no matter how long, but only by a spiritual journey, a journey of one inch, very arduous and humbling and joyful, by which we arrive at the ground at our own feet, and learn to be at home. It is a journey we can make only by the acceptance of mystery and of mystification—by yielding to the condition that what we have expected is not there.

I think this describes a metamorphosis perfectly, as if our imaginal cells have consumed us and are forming us anew. Yet how often do you rush past or delay this process within yourself?

How often does a reliance on intellect get in the way of the depth of change that's possible for us? Often I wonder if the magical part of being human is sadly being picked over in favor of the latest influencer strategies for being the best you. The force of the intellect is too violent for the process of coming home to ourselves. You cannot rely on will to change or force your life to take a different shape. You must rely on your soul, which offers a different pace or rhythm as you chart the course of your own map.

Are we ready to arrive home, to find our authentic self, to align with our soul?

Failing to look inward is settling for the status quo. It's settling for life as a caterpillar and refusing to fly. Regardless of your choice to inquire within or not, the unconscious is having its way with you.

What remains unexplored inside you may be showing up within your organization in a confining or non-beneficial way. To bring it out of the shadows, it's important to bring light to what's happening for you, what you're really up to in those moments, in order to move towards awakening. At Reboot, we call this "using the work to do our work."

A practice of radical self-inquiry allows you to notice what happens in your experience from a different vantage point—one of curiosity. For example, you may discover that your company is a reaction to a childhood trauma/drama or designed to save a younger version of yourself. An important question to get curious about is: What are you creating and for whom?

"Reclaiming our shadow not only brings personal reward, it also helps support transformation in our teams, organizations, communities—and beyond," wrote Elle Harrison in her book *Wild Courage: A Journey of Transformation for You and Your Business*. Working with our shadow can bring up questions that take us on a journey of transformation into what Elle calls courageous leadership:

> It's not an easy journey, but the rewards are immense. As we venture through the shadows of our unconscious, we come deeper into our selves. We make contact with our

essence, and we allow it to re-express itself in new and creative ways. We discover a new center of gravity: our inner truth, our authentic and wild self—our soul. Realigning our life and work around our wild self, we come "home" to ourselves—and we find renewed passion, purpose, and meaning in our leadership, life, and work.

The result of looking inward, of "doing your inner work," is essential to transforming more than just ourselves. Our personal journeys ripple through our work in the world, as Elle adds:

> Engaging in a personal journey of transformation is perhaps our most powerful way of supporting these wider changes. As Albert Einstein said, "We cannot solve the problem with the consciousness that created the problem. We must learn to see the world anew." When we integrate our shadow, we do indeed see the world anew. With our fresh eyes, we find new insight, new innovation and radically creative solutions to the challenges of our time. Ripples of our own personal journeys reach out across politics, education, business, the environment, healthcare, and every other human system, paving the way for a vibrant and sustainable future. These changes begin in the inner world of each leader. They begin with you.

Radical self-inquiry is part of a continual practice of growth and self-actualization. Coming home to the ground at our own feet, we can see so much more of ourselves, and heed the changes with awareness. From there, with practice, we notice our own process of becoming. We can sense our wholeness: our light that we willingly shine outward, and all the stuff we're not proud of that we put down into the deep dark place behind us. We see more clearly what parts of us (beliefs, habits, personas) are old, not serving us, and are ready to die. We can see where we are resistant or holding ourselves back from awakening more and more into our own lives. And we can begin to let life meet us, as we emerge more fully than ever before.

It's a journey best done with a guide. Someone to hold you not too tight—not too loose. Someone who will keep you at your edge, but not force a methodology down your throat. Someone who can help you hear your own heart. Sometimes life does this for us, if we allow it. If we can be present for it, we emerge eventually with brilliant, glistening wings.

The Act to Follow: Becoming More Difficult to Disrupt

For transitions where an old part of us was shed and a newer us emerged, the successful second acts are a result of us setting out more true to ourselves. Through career changes, divorce, or returning to work after raising kids, we can step into that next act more wholly, more holistically, with all the authenticity we've got at this stage in our life.

We bring all that we've learned, all that we know, everything worth keeping close, and a keen attunement to that part of us that knows quietly and resolutely without needing to ask for approval, validation, permission, or recognition. Ask yourself these questions:

> ➤ How do you want to be, now, as you look at the act you're in the midst of or the new act you're moving into?

> ➤ How do you want to relate to work?

> ➤ What life would you like to create for yourself?

> ➤ How are you directing the course of your own life?

THE PRACTICE: PERSONAL GROWTH IS ESSENTIAL TO BUSINESS GROWTH

Unless you grow, your business won't grow. When you grow as a human, your leadership changes. What matters to *you* changes. Your way of being changes, which changes how you show up to your life and for others. When you grow, you free up those around you to grow as well, including your team.

We can show up with the fullness of our weary and broken hearts alongside our gumption (or whatever gumption we might feel is left in us) and learn about ourselves. We can suspend our ways of thinking long enough to change our mind and mend our hearts in the process. We've seen it time and again with entrepreneurs willing to look at work as a place to achieve their fullest selves.

Perhaps, along the way on our entrepreneurial paths, we can show up for people as much as we showed up for the profits. Perhaps we can show up not for what we think we'll get out of something, but to receive greater lessons from the experience. Maybe we let our psychic armor down long enough for something to get through to us. Perhaps we pull the wool back from our eyes and see ourselves and our lives more clearly, free of self-deception and delusion.

Think back over the past six months, or past twelve months, or even back to when you began your company:

> Who were you then?
> Who are you now?
> What do you know differently?
> How do you know differently?
> How have you grown?

Part V

LAYING A FOUNDATION OF TRUST

AN ALTERNATIVE TO FEAR-BASED LEADERSHIP: A BRIEF CASE FOR LOVE

One of the questions we muse on here at Reboot HQ is: What is it to lead from a place of love versus a place of fear? After we posed that question at an offsite, after a long pause, one of our clients said: "It's so much harder to lead with love."

The first step of leadership requires personal growth and learning a more functional way to be in the world, with each other, and with ourselves. It's an inside job. This is how better humans make better leaders. We meet the challenges of life and entrepreneurship with the skills we have and what we've learned about our way of being. In this way, love indeed makes damn good business.

"The biggest impediment to humane workplaces is the unsorted baggage we carry, the wounds we have," Jerry noted to me over dinner a while back. "We fear that our past negative experiences (from work or otherwise) will be reenacted. We're therefore too afraid—too afraid to trust." When we let those negative experiences cloud our present sense of things, we start defending against them in ways ruled by fear and acting out onto others.

Fear-based leadership usually occurs when we are acting from a place of contraction, often in the form of defensive behavior (because defending is what humans do when they are in fear). Some of these behaviors include withdrawal, withholding, and projection. Other ways this may show up is bullying, emotional outbursts, and shutting others down for disturbing the status quo. Some defenses are loud and obvious, while others are quieter—such as withdrawal and withholding. Whenever any of these behaviors show up, they are almost always originating from a place of fear and an attempt to protect. We often fall into our adaptive patterns when there's stress, conflict, or uncertainty. When we feel under threat or don't feel safe, we resort to a whole range of behaviors that we used to cope with those feelings when we were younger.

Not only does this affect how we show up as individuals, but it also greatly influences how we are able to show up with others as part of a group. In fear-based leadership, we see a lack of relational and environmental awareness and less self-awareness in general. Folks won't reveal their feelings and may not pause to parse them out. What can happen in fear-based workplace cultures is scapegoating, caretaking, and a lack of direct and transparent communication.

Leadership that comes from love still has conflict and hard conversations and emotions such as anger. The major difference is there's an emotional maturity that can hold it all in a humane way.

Leading from love takes proactive cultivating. It takes tending to. It takes mindfulness. Here's why: the evolution of the brain is such that the base level of the operating system is fight or flight (survival), which is where fear starts. All other levels of the brain were built on top of that, with love coming from the prefrontal cortex. Love, then, becomes accessible after traveling through the entire brain stack. Thus if you react quickly, you react from lower in the brain stack (fear). If you can pause and be mindful by taking that space between stimulus and response, then your brain can get to love and respond from that place. That is potent growth.

Love means clear boundaries and knowing where you stand. It means knowing what you need and tending to your own well-being. It's taking responsibility for your actions and your emotional regulation. It's knowing the difference between the subconscious self and the higher self, between the false self and the authentic self, and continually uncovering their many layers. Love is the freedom to be you, to speak your truth in a way that does not hurt others, and to consciously create your life by making choices that are fully integrated with your purpose and values.

Love doesn't mean being selfless to the point that you disappear. It means learning how to be fully you—not shrinking, not relying on your fears and insecurities, and not being shut down and invulnerable—so that you can show up to life, others, and issues as they meet you.

Building on this understanding of love, I invite you to investigate further with the following questions:

> What do you know about your adaptive patterns from childhood? What did love mean in your family of origin? Fill in the blank: In order to be loved or feel safety and belonging as a kid, I needed to _____.

> What fears arise in you when it comes to your relationships? Where do you feel scared to say what you need to say or be who you are?

> What does love mean to you in the context of relationships? In the context of work?

> Describe relationships you've been in that were equitable, unconditional, and in which you felt seen and heard. In what relationships do you feel loved and celebrated for who you are?

> How can you show up in ways that are not fear-based in your working life, in your work relationships, and in your leadership?

THE SPACE BETWEEN

My dad let me use my college fund to buy a horse when I was eleven. I commend him for that decision, even though much to his chagrin one horse led to two, and before I knew it, I had a barn full. (That's how horse-math works.) While I've had many amazing mentors in my life, I've always said that my best teachers were my horses. Their lesson plans consisted of a silent conversation between species. In that space between my world and theirs, I learned about relating to an Other with an ancient language, one in which rapport, communication, boundaries, and emotional congruence created safety and trust.

Trust and respect were the foundation of our work together. With an ever-increasing awareness of each other, there was ease at play in the space between and a refined communication between us. We could sense each other. We knew when the other was tense and what was needed to return to calm and connection, so we could be with each other and flow together. It became a co-creative relationship, which felt like a burst of poetry in which $1 + 1 = 3$. Much like watching accomplished dancers move across the floor together with utter grace, in the synergistic relationship between my horses and me, the whole was greater than the sum of its parts.

The horses taught me about the importance of this dance, and not only what it takes to play well with others, but what it means to create and be part of a third, much greater thing. In fact, I wrote an entire master's thesis on this very phenomenon.

Yet working with the horses wasn't all sugar cubes and sweet-grass. There were plenty of days when trust was lost and the connection between us seemed gone; when my patience was tested and it showed; when either of our anxieties got in the way of our coming together; and moments when both horse and I looked at each other like we were from opposing planets with no direct line between us nor an interest to find one. At those times, I felt marooned.

With horses, if something's not working, something is not working. Forcing the matter doesn't create a positive result. There must be an opening for change to happen. And that shift had to come from inside one of us. We needed to show up differently for each other. Most of the time, that started with me. Hello, radical self-inquiry. (Horses are human whisperers, after all.)

Oh, relationships. If only human relationships were different, easier perhaps. Even with all our sophisticated frontal lobe activity and laudable opposable thumbs, they're not. Our relationships are our mirrors; and rapport, communication, self-awareness, safety, and trust are all still part of the whole deal that make playing in the space between possible.

I've been thinking about this dance that co-founders find themselves in. When two or more people come together to work on and in a company, they are more than the sum of their parts. Each individual who joins in becomes part of an "us" entity. As a third much greater thing, this us needs tending to just as each individual needs tending to in order to best serve and support the creative capacity of the whole endeavor.

How graceful can that us be?

Fostering a sense of trust and safety creates openings ripe with co-creative collaborative possibilities. As leadership expert Warren Bennis reminds us, "Trust is the lubrication that makes it possible for organizations to work." When we trust each other, we feel safe to show up as our best selves and make great things happen.

When stress is present in any person or interaction, those dynamics constrict the possibility for creativity between individuals, undermining the effectiveness of the us. Prolonged and unresolved stress creates toxicity and zaps energy within teams and companies. While stress can't be avoided, it can be met as an opportunity for a shift in perception that will lead to clarity within an individual or between people.

Wouldn't it be great if we took time to think about how we wanted to work together; if we took time to learn about what our partner needed to return to center in a moment of stress; if each individual of a team felt safe enough to bring their whole self to the table, to be amazing together and to co-create the best work of their lives?

What if we had a useful blueprint for working together effectively: a tool we could use to mindfully custom design what we want to do and how we want to be together? Such a tool would be a reference point to return to in order to restore connection and co-creative capacity for relationships based on trust, appreciation, and respect. If teams designed their relationship to each other and around the opportunity in front of them, they could grow together—as friends, business partners, and as leaders in their roles—based on how they chose to design the partnership. It all starts with a subversively simple question—What would you like?—and is followed by a commitment to consciously co-create that into being.

EXPANDING OUR POTENTIAL

I once wrote in an old blog that "relationships are the new ashram." Meaning that once you enter one, you'll be meeting many opportunities to do your inner work, no trips to India necessary. The work—*your* work—presents itself in any relationship, not only in those of the romantic kind.

One of the more difficult things about relationships is this understanding that as individuals each of us has an entirely different map of reality, caused by years of experiences that have imprinted our neurology just so—and uniquely so. No two human maps are the same. The hardware may be similar, but when it comes to the programming and the code, to each their own.

Because of this, when two people come together and share in conversation or a co-creative adventure like a startup, it is an interesting chiasma. Yet it's in that shared space between individuals that a lot of magic can happen. A lot of healing can happen, too, if people come together mindfully.

In his book *How to Be an Adult in Relationships*, David Richo reminds us that the word mindfulness is a translation of Sanskrit words meaning "attend" and "stay." He also notes that when you pay attention and stay with someone in their feelings—in their here-and-now predicament—accepting someone in this serene and present way, shifts occur in each of you, and both begin to discover the skillful means to be more appreciative and supportive.

How mindful you are in the relationships that are most key to your work and life has positively life-changing implications. By staying with and attending to what comes up for you and the person sitting across from you, you're creating space to become aware of what is presenting itself and to actively choose another way to be.

Consider this soundbite of data on the human OS: Our conscious mind processes information at two thousand bits per second, and our subconscious mind processes information at eleven million bits per second.

That's a lot of information running what you say, think, and do that you're not even aware of. But relationships can provide a mirror to catch glimpses of all that your subconscious isn't showing you. (Paying attention to what stresses you is another clue to follow.) Becoming aware of what's presenting itself brings it onto the stage of the conscious mind so you can see it, learn from it, and choose to speak, think, or do something different.

Learning to do that with yourself is one thing. Building that awareness with a partner is a wholly other barrel of monkeys. Yet without this self-awareness, and this relational awareness, our pasts become present and we can sabotage whatever it is we are wanting to create together.

There's no need to find a relationship therapist. Start simply. In living and working with others, it helps to know some basic data from them: What are you like on a good day? What are you like when you're stressed, and how will I know it? What do you need in those moments? Be willing to pause and use this information in the practice fields of your relationships in your personal life and within your organization.

Relating mindfully is key to expanding and realizing our potential as individuals and as organizations. In thinking about your relationships and what you'd like to create, spend a few moments with this advice from James Hollis's *What Matters Most: Living a More Considered Life:* "All of us have to ask this simple but piercing question of our relationships, our affiliations, our professions, our politics, and our theology: 'Does this path, this choice, make me larger or smaller?'"

THE GIFTS OF RELATIONSHIP

The paradox of relationship will always be that rather than solve our problems for us, relationship brings us new problems, new complexities, but that we also grow immensely from these problems, these complexities. In short, the greatest gift of relationship proves to be that as the result of encountering each other, we are obliged to grow larger than we had planned.

—James Hollis

Spare yourself a navel-gazing trip to India to dive into epic dimensions of self-awareness and personal growth. Your best opportunity for such growth is hanging with the person you happen to be with.

When I was musing on relationships and moving through the dissolution of my marriage, I asked my therapist, "What does an ideal relationship look like?" He took a second to gather his thoughts and replied:

> Once a commitment is made, the main theme in a healthy relationship should be about personal growth. The fundamental concept also has to do with purpose. If the purpose of partnership is to have the other person make us happy, we are in for a rough ride because they will inevitably disappoint in one way or another. If the purpose of life is the fulfillment of consciousness—and we are intentionally, consciously using partnership as a way to confront and

work with our limitations and complex personality structures—ah!—then we have a chance.

Just like my therapist suggested that a romantic partnership is the
way to grow, so it is with our co-founder relationships.

This is the truth of relationships, in all the forms they may
take: they are our best chance at conscious growth because they
are a mirror for what comes up for us—our shadow and light, our
projections and assumptions. Being in partnership shows where
our inner work needs some inner working. In a sense, you are the
result of your practice, and the reflections you get while interacting
with others can give you keen insight into your edges.

The most successful partnerships are based on a rich bed of
trust. It's the kind of trust you'd equate with a well-performing
baseball team: everyone shows up in their role, and there's trust
that someone is going to catch the ball at first base. There's no
second-guessing, no conversation needed. It's a well-understood
and well-oiled machine of beings in union around the same goals,
values, and focus. That level of togetherness takes lots of practice
and a high level of commitment from each individual.

Relationships are crucibles for our deepest inner work if we
remain open and committed to the premise and practice of showing
up and doing our work. The reward of that alchemical fire is the
emergence of your inner gold.

But it certainly isn't easy. David Richo writes in *How to Be
an Adult in Relationships* that "the commitment to work through
problems as they arise is the only sign that we truly want full intimacy." A large part of that commitment is our willingness to be
vulnerable in our work in the presence of another. That level of
work can only happen when we feel trust and a loving presence.
Richo puts forth what he calls the Five A's and their importance in
the practice of being adult in relationship with others and yourself: attention, acceptance, appreciation, affection, and allowing.

Together, they are the components of love that make a relationship a truly caring connection.

To feel into these five A's, consider how you show up in relationships based on mindfulness—and the opposites of mindfulness: fear, demand, expectation, judgement, and control. The difference looks and feels quite different. Being mindful in relationships means being attentive, accepting, appreciative, and allowing for what is. There's a clear presence at the helm when you show up this way. When we are not present, and when we can't be mindfully aware, we exhibit a whole realm of behaviors such as poor listening or outright ignoring, being unavailable, fear of what someone might say. We may be full of criticism and judgement. We may be passive or actively aggressive. We may try to control, make demands, be manipulative, or at worst selfish and abusive.

Becoming mindful of how you are being in relationships is the path to embodying a loving presence for the ones you're with. (My animal companions have always had that loving presence in spades. They make the Five A's look easy.)

Where do you find yourself most often in your relationship with your co-founder and yourself? What happens to the feeling tone* of your working partnership when you're acting from mindfulness versus fixed mindsets? When I am operating from the mindsets of ego, I leave no space for the person I'm with to feel safe, heard, loved, and able to flourish. I leave no space for their heart to show up in full. I can create potential for harm rather than cultivating a space for healing and connection.

Self-awareness is a prerequisite for a path of continued personal growth and discovery. It's what allows partners to weather storms and sea changes, to witness and support each other in our own

---

* Feeling tone, at its most basic definition, is the sensation of either pleasant, unpleasant, or neutral. Practicing mindfulness of feeling tone allows us to pause before reacting to a feeling in a habitual or unwise way.

process of becoming. It also allows each individual to tend to the hearth of the relationship.

What's possible here is a maturity in relating that can't be done from a place of insecurity or self-centeredness, where we have no chance of succeeding. When we can embrace what the mirror of relationship reflects back to us, and seize our work as a perpetual practice, we can then receive the greatest gift of encountering each other as Hollis notes, and we are obliged to grow larger than we had planned.

RADICAL HONESTY

My voice is born repeatedly in the fields of uncertainty.

—Terry Tempest Williams

One of our facilitators reminded me of this simple truth a few years ago: "The basic unit of work is a conversation." While so much of work hinges on voice, I have abandoned mine over the years out of fear that it's not safe to say what I need to say. But it's not always easy to quiet that little voice inside me. I've learned and relearned how much it certainly bears many truths worth uttering.

I grew up in a home where communication wasn't always straight shootin'. Emotions weren't talked about—or received—in an adult way, and there were some things you just didn't talk about even if everyone knew about it. That kind of incongruence was unnerving as a child developing her senses and learning to trust herself. When someone told me something that didn't seem to match the feeling in the air, my beacon of inner knowing was thrown off. My sense of "But why does it not feel quite right?" was a hard thing to reconcile as a kid, and made me a bit of the straight shooter in the family. If no one else was going to say what was really going on, it would almost surely come out of my mouth exactly as I saw it, much to the shock of my family members.

Later in grade school, one of my teachers gave each of us bookmarks with the meaning and origin of our names on them. Allison, of Irish-Gaelic origin, meant "little truthful one." Some part of me took that as an aspiration to live up to, but I didn't always trust my own voice and what I really wanted to say.

Even if I couldn't put words to what was happening, I could usually tell when something wasn't right by how it felt in my body. When I was exasperated as to why no one was talking about something, that vexation created tension in me until what was really going on was named and voiced. (Some accounts didn't get resolved or squared up until I was well into my thirties.)

It has taken me years to use the words "this doesn't feel right to me" out loud, to name the dissonant feeling I was having about a situation. There was also part of me that wanted to trust what was happening, what people were saying, what was being presented as the whole story, without asking questions, prodding further, or saying anything against the grain. I call that my gut-override capacity, which can show up in work situations. I can be sitting in a meeting, listening to what's being said, and a slew of questions arise in my inside-my-head-voice that would further the conversation—perhaps be really provocative—yet the words hesitate to leave my mouth in the moment.

In her book *When Women Were Birds: Fifty-Four Variations on Voice*, Terry Tempest Williams writes, "When we don't listen to our intuition, we abandon our souls. And we abandon our souls because we are afraid if we don't, others will abandon us."

A few years ago, I worked with a presentation coach on finding my voice. I had to get over feeling like I was going to be burned at the stake for speaking out loud. We were working on call-and-response articulations of various consonant and vowel sound combinations, and locating the origin of sound deep in my abdomen, when I became aware of that place where voice began and where it wanted to silence itself before it escaped into the wild.

Somewhere in the tangle of "this doesn't feel right" and my capacity to override my gut intuition, my straight-shootin' Annie Oakley perspective gets muddled with self-doubt and smothered in fear of stating her truth. Even if I have the words to articulate the feelings and name the incongruities I see and hear, they get stopped up in a jumble at my vocal cords out of fear that they are too powerful to be heard.

By keeping my voice on lockdown, with my fears of being too much or saying something someone doesn't want to hear holding the key, I'm not really being honest at all. When I keep how I really feel on the inside, and not in my outside voice, it throws a kink in my ability to show up and relate authentically. Mostly, that keeps me unheard and unseen—complicit in creating a few of the things I say I don't want.

Being radically honest is a door we each must walk through in our lives. It's a powerful move that starts in our conversations, and how honest they are—at work, in our relationships, with our loved ones.

In the spirit of radical honesty, I invite you to ask yourself:

> Where do you give your power away?

> When, where, and how do you silence your voice?

> In what ways has your silence kept you safe?

> Where and in what relationships do you hold back?

> What do you think would happen if you spoke up?

> What is the risk of not saying what you need to say?

BUILDING BRIDGES

Safety is a necessary component of what makes us comfortable to show up wholly as ourselves. It's a necessary component of our work environments, especially our co-founder relationships.

We often go through our days inadvertently threatening others' sense of safety by denying or hiding our emotions—or worse, *erupting* with emotion. Or we exacerbate a workmate's upregulated moments by our own nonverbal communication, or our reactions (or lack thereof). Sometimes our unnamed feelings can come out sideways, in ways that hurt. And before you know it, someone may be feeling quite red in an amygdala hijack moment.

We all react differently in these moments, poised with different defenses. When these defenses and wired reactions shut us down from an open communication stance in which we might have hearty *con*versations, we can only head into *non*-versation territory—unless we have the awareness and mindfulness to navigate these moments. It's hard to communicate when emotions are triggered like hot wires, or bottled up and unvoiced.

This mindfulness of our own reactivity is essential to being in relationship to another. We each have our own bag of "stuff"—the ways we learned to communicate and how we handle our emotions—that shows up in the verbal transactions the days call for at work and home. Failure to tend to tense moments fraught with emotion, either said or unsaid, festers. And moving right past them may not be wise, as those tensions can linger only to come up later, possibly more intense or filled with resentment.

The good news is that we also have the capacity to make our colleagues feel safe. We can help them regulate their inner state by coming to understand what they need in those moments when they may be shut down, in code-red mode, or any other expression of a fear state. Relational repair helps others heal their own wounding that happened in relationship. If we can lean in to repair, we can build trust.

Our work-pace may not seem to offer us the time or space needed to air feelings that arise or to skillfully name them. But making time for these conversations can be a game-changer for your company, especially if you are a co-founder. From the first conversations at the genesis of your company, and onward as your team grows, learning what your co-founder and co-workers value and need in communication is key to supporting them through the ups and downs of your daily and weekly work adventures.

While deep into Brené Brown's book *Braving the Wilderness*, I ran across a definition of trust that perfectly weaves together vulnerability and personal values. Brown quotes Charles Feltman, author of *The Thin Book of Trust*, who describes trust as "choosing to risk making something you value vulnerable to another person's actions." He then describes distrust as "deciding what is important to me is not safe with this person in this situation (or any situation)."

Our point of view is informed by our unique sensibilities and how we know the world. If we don't trust our partners and co-workers, how much of ourselves do we bottle up when big issues arise, when we have perspective and feelings to share? What do we sense from our environment that shuts us down? What do we need to feel safe?

The responses to these questions differ for each of us. We have all come to our emotional needs and expressions (or tendency for bottled expressions) honestly via our varied histories wired into our equally varied neurologies. So many of these imprints began in the first minutes to years of our lives as our caregivers assured, reassured, or dismissed our very existence in their responses to us. (I offer this as a reminder to be gentle with ourselves, and those around us when they are in an upregulated or triggered state.)

Despite our differences, there are several bedrock elements that make us feel safe with each other. In her book, Brown describes the fundamentals she considers essential to trusting others with her BRAVING acronym: Boundaries, Reliability, Accountability, Vault (respecting privacy and confidentiality), Integrity, Non-judgement, and Generosity.

When one or more of these is missing from an interaction with others, how do you feel? How do you exercise these qualities to show up for your relationships at home and at work?

We build bridges with each other when we can provide safety and space for others to show up, say what they need to say, voice feelings, and talk about what's happening as it's arising. When another person does the same for us, we feel safe. These baseline qualities serve as a general orientation to what is required of others and ourselves. However, there are specifics that each of us have— that we came to honestly—that make a difference in our communication styles and what we need in various moments to come back to center and feel safe. Uncovering what we need when we are angry, scared, sad, and insecure is a great exercise for ourselves, so we can recognize where we are at and perhaps let those around us know what we need and what best serves us in our triggered or upregulated or feely moments.

Consider the following:

> What's the qualitative feel you want to have when working with your team?

> What are the commitments you'll make to support each other in coming back to center when things are upregulated?

> Culture is the sum of the behaviors in an organization. What are the behaviors that will move you towards the collective goals your company is aiming for?

A GOOD EAR

*The beauty of listening is that those who are listened
to start feeling accepted, start taking their words more
seriously and discovering their own true selves.*

—Henry Nouwen

Long before Reboot, the people in my life used to tell me I was a
good listener. I had no idea what they were talking about, but lots
of folks in my life—including a few strangers—would open up
to me pretty readily. Generally, people talked, I listened, and they
felt better. I have also been on the receiving end of that, too many
times to enumerate, and grateful for every ear that's been there to
hear me process at various moments in my life when things were
turbulent, transitioning, or happening all at once. A good ear is
a priceless gift, and good listening is a healing art form we're all
capable of mastering—within ourselves and for each other.

Listening, however, wasn't always easy—nor, looking back, was
I always good at it. There were many times my "I'm just here listening to you" stance was jostled: I would become attached to their
stories, get triggered in my own ways depending on the content, feel
all of *their* feelings, feel my own feelings in reaction to their feelings,
or any of the myriad ways in which being a listener goes awry.

When that happened, my stuff would get in the way of their
voice, trampling that sensitive space of receiving-listening and
shutting them down to some degree in the process. I'm sure we've

all felt this at one time or another. There you are in the depths of recounting what's up for you to a rapt audience of one, and then comes an interruption, interjection, a quick solution, or pointed question that usurps your space and your voice.

It's a feat for us humans to be a good ear. True listening is generous. It's attuned to both our listener and ourselves. True listening requires the listener to have the inner strength to be present enough for the speaker that they feel seen, heard, and free to share in that un-cramped space. So few people know how to truly listen. It's hard to hear the rough stuff of someone's experience if our own stuff gets agitated and activated. If we can't be generous, our stuff gets in the way and we end up not listening, which can feel pretty bad for the person who needs a big ear.

Listening involves putting ourselves and our own interests aside for a bit. It involves getting curious about the other person, as if we could step onto the map of their reality for a moment to see what they see, feel what they feel, and understand how things are oriented and structured from their place in space. All of that would require us, as listeners, to let go of any presumption that our own map of the world is the only map of reality. When we listen, we're sitting at the edge of uncharted territory—that of the other person's experience—despite how similar it may feel to us as their story draws parallels with our own.

As life comes at us fast and furiously, the trick to slowing down through the rough spots is being able to be with what's happening and all the accompanying feelings, even if they are uncomfortable. Being alone with our thoughts and feelings can make us feel bottled up, which can keep us feeling tense and perhaps unclear. It can keep us from being able to move forward until we sort things out for ourselves. Having a big ear helps. In those moments, it helps to know we're not alone, to have someone to listen, someone to bear witness to how hard/scary/crazy/sad/maddening things have been.

Slowing down to ask and listen is a potent offering. Just by being present enough, brave enough, and compassionate enough to reach out and get curious about someone else, we give them the gift of being witnessed, seen, and heard in a way that validates their experience and their humanness.

How can we be that patient, spacious, and giving for each other? How can we develop our good ear? One tool is to ask open, honest questions—questions that we don't already have the answers to (or expectations of what the right answer *should* be). This is one that if used often enough becomes second nature to you. The other tool is to listen more—in other words, be silent. When the person has completed their thoughts, then ask another good, open question. Here in this space, without rushing to fix, we give people a chance to hear themselves, and their own inner stirrings.

As I explore in the essay "Red–Yellow–Green" on page 240, "How are you?" is one of the simplest questions to ask of each other, when we're really ready to listen. It sometimes feels that I'm really asking, "How is your heart today, right now, in this moment?" How often do you ask that of friends, colleagues, your partner, your children; and how often do you sit back and listen, truly hearing all that they have to say?

Listening requires an open silence, free from criticism, defense, or a closed-off withdrawal. So much happens when we hold space for that kind of silence, both for the listener and interpersonally in the space between us.

And for those us being truly listened to, when given the space to process we hear ourselves in the silence of a good listener, allowing things to become congruent in our body-mind-heart, as if all the thoughts and reams of feelings—named, unnamed, and unnamable—congeal into more clarity or calm. We can see more of what is happening within, around, and for us as we hear our own articulations. Ultimately, by being listened to, we feel more connected to ourselves.

CONGRUENCE

Hard times arouse an instinctive desire for authenticity.

—Coco Chanel

Jerry often says that trust is a by-product of the value of being authentic. But how do you commit to being an authentic leader, in success and failure, while you scale your business at the same time? What's at stake if you don't?

Trust is a firm belief in the reliability, truth, ability, or strength of someone or something in which we place our confidence. Trust in our organizations undergirds success. Trust is what empowers teams to manifest a company's vision. Without trust, our teams and companies are in jeopardy. Lack of trust will derail any attempts to improve company culture. And if you've ever been in that situation, you know it feels awful. It's stressful. No one is saying what needs to be said. There's fear, anxiety, tension, and conflict. Meanwhile, the product is going nowhere.

In his classic leadership fable *The Five Dysfunctions of a Team*, Patrick Lencioni notes, "Trust is the foundation of real teamwork. And so, the first dysfunction is a failure on the part of team members to understand and open up to one another. And if that sounds touchy-feely, let me explain, because there is nothing soft about it. It is an absolutely critical part of building a team. In fact, it's probably *the* most critical." He adds, "Remember teamwork begins by building trust. And the only way to do that is to overcome our need for invulnerability."

Growing up, I learned a lot about trust—and what it takes to establish it—from my horses. When a horse trusts you, he looks to you for leadership. That's the quintessential quality of horsemanship (read: leadership), because without trust, a horse-rider relationship lacks connection and is instead fraught with anxiety, fear, and conflict. When that happens, neither critter feels safe and will react defensively in an act of self-preservation. It's hard times in the relationship department. Ultimately, you don't get anywhere.

Horses are barometers for how authentic and real you are being in their presence. They have this incredible built-in bullsh*t meter and know when you're posturing. In their presence when I was emotionally congruent, they could trust me. In other words, if I was feeling sad on the inside and fully aware of it, it showed in my exterior differently than if I was trying to hide it. As long as I was congruent, they were right there with me. No tension. No stress. Whereas, if I was feeling one thing internally and presenting another, the horses would be on edge, anxious; they would show physiological signs of fear because they didn't feel safe around me. I was perceived as a threat and they would rather be anywhere but next to me. Their reaction was honest feedback on my interior and exterior alignment. I learned quickly to become attuned to myself and how I was showing up, so I could also be attuned to my horse. Only then would any tension between us subside, so we could begin working together as partners.

Horses are prey animals, meaning they are susceptible to becoming dinner to predators such as mountain lions, wolves, coyotes, or bears. Their entire nervous system is wired to sense threats in the environment and, as such, they are inherently sensitive animals. They can sense when a mountain lion is close and even more so when a big cat is trying to look like a rock. Their systems know the incongruity of the furry rock with whiskers because their life depends on that level of sensory acuity. As humans our brains may have taken new shape further down the evolutionary branches, yet we have this critter neurology within our wiring and can sense incongruity in others. Think about it for a moment: How do you know you can't trust someone or something? Something feels off, right?

Imagine how your team feels if trust is missing from your culture, if they don't feel safe to say what they need to say, or to name the elephant in the room. Interior and exterior alignment is critical in leadership. It creates the basic conditions to make people feel safe. When we feel safe, we can relax and do our best work because we're not looking out for someone or something to put us on the defensive.

The reason we trust each other is because we're being real with each other. "Great teams do not hold back with one another. They are unafraid to air their dirty laundry. They admit their mistakes, their weaknesses, and their concerns without fear of reprisal," writes Lencioni. "Politics is when people choose their words and actions based on how they want others to react rather than based on what they really think."

By maintaining your emotional congruency, you show up more authentically and build your presence and effectiveness as a leader. Allowing yourself to be yourself gives others permission to be themselves. If embodying the values of authenticity are not part and parcel of your culture, somebody must go first. Someone has to have the audacity to be themselves, to be honest, to be real. In a culture that feels toxic, that's a courageous move.

Being authentic feels like the right thing to do. And once you find it, it's as if something trues up in you and all of you aligns— head, voice, heart, gut, and feet.

Sometimes I sense a deep questioning about being authentic in our working lives, as if some voice inside us utters disbelief against that voice within us that speaks with gentle clarity and urges us to say what we need to say. "I can't be real / be honest / be me, can I?" I see this question asked silently in the faces of clients all the time, and wonder what stops us from being authentic. Perhaps it's a fear we all hold deep within us about not belonging: the fear of being unloved, abandoned, and hurt for being who we are.

And yet it's critical that we show up authentically in our work and life. Being congruent demands that we be real with ourselves and others, that we align our inner states with our outer states. If you, as a leader, can show up this way consistently, you can lead with the kind of love that will ripple in positive ways throughout the organization.

Now that's something I can ride along with.

SHOW ME YOU CARE

*If you could only sense how important you are to the lives
of those you meet; how important you can be to the people
you may never even dream of. There is something of yourself
that you leave at every meeting with another person.*

—Fred Rogers

In a not-so-distant past life, I worked in a series of workplaces that
felt awful—stressful, tense, and anxiety inducing—for a slew of
reasons. The organization was disorganized. The leadership was at
odds with each other. Roles and expectations and communications
were unclear. My co-workers could also see the clusterf*ck at every
juncture. At my lowest points, I felt I had to check the best parts
of me at the door when I walked into the office. Nothing felt more
soul-sucking, yet I kept showing up to it…until I didn't.

When things at one company started to go awry, I brought
up issues to my boss directly, who was also the owner-founder of
the company. Of course, I'd also fielded plenty of conversations
within the team about many of the issues that we all saw and for
some reason put up with for a little too long. I compiled my notes
and my chutzpah in an email to my boss, asking if we could meet.
He agreed willingly, and we talked for roughly two hours about
the issues that I and the team were running into, where the stress
points were, where things felt out of alignment, etc. While I wanted
to change things for the better—for the company—these issues

were also coming up against operational and strategic decisions upon which my boss had been running the company for a while. He listened to everything I had to say, asked great questions, and before we walked away with action items, he said to me: "I really admire your bravery for talking to me about these things." He was genuine. I felt relief.

Years later at a different organization, I found myself in a weekly finance meeting with my CEO. We were looking at the numbers, which was anxiety inducing at the time, and considering the current P&L and the two-month forecast compared with our aspirational goals. When I voiced my feelings about what we were looking at, "These numbers scare me a bit," the CEO turned to me and said curtly, "I don't need you to get emotional about this." I clammed up. Right, I mean, who has time for emotionality? This meeting was no place for being human in the face of spreadsheets. After that encounter, some part of me felt even more afraid to say what I needed to say with people I worked with every day. I always felt like if I cried—much less simply voiced a feeling—that my job would be on the line. I'm sure I wasn't the only one to feel that way.

It's hard working for someone else, and it's hard working in a toxic organization, when you don't feel you have a voice or can do anything to make a positive change. I felt pinched, cut off, divided. Somewhere in the anxiety stressing through my veins and the cloud of fear I lived in at the office, the fear that silenced my voice and dulled my chutzpah, I was divided between my inner convictions and what I witnessed or felt I couldn't speak about. I felt powerless.

What can you do as a non-positional leader in a work environment that's dysfunctional? How can you find meaningful work that supports your well-being in an organization that feels toxic or denies your humanity? Our best work happens when we're at ease, not stressed out and drowning in anxiety and fear about the status of our belonging. During a 2016 Reboot podcast conversation, Parker Palmer touched on an important aspect of this that addresses not only an organization's people, but also creativity and innovation. Palmer brings to our attention the importance of relational trust—the interpersonal social exchanges that take place in a group setting—when he says, "Relational trust is built on movements of the human heart such as empathy, commitment, compassion, patience, and the capacity to forgive."

After all, the fundamental unit of work is a conversation.

In my examples, the first company had more relational trust than the second. In the first company, I felt safe enough to talk to my boss about what was happening for me versus the other in which I felt as if anything I said, even in confidence, would be turned against me. In one, I felt like someone *had* my back. In the other, I felt like I had to *watch* my back.

We talk a lot about the notion of shadow in leadership. When a leader is operating from their shadow, I always say that it's like their disowned unconscious stuff is coming out sideways and the people in their lives become collateral damage. When we use the organization to project our issues, recreate family of origin stories and dynamics, do our unfinished inner work (unconsciously, narcissistically), and fail to recognize what we're creating, the organization's toxicity tends to increase. Therefore, as a leader, there's a moral and ethical responsibility to be aware of one's shadow—and to prioritize relational trust as part of the team.

People who are heavily shadowed tend to also be heavily defended, which makes approaching them with feedback challenging, especially if that feedback comes from someone in a non-positional role. To make that kind of open, honest communication work among colleagues requires a culture that creates safe space for that kind of feedback organization-wide. This is a culture that builds, maintains, and tends to trustworthy relations. A culture that can listen to and hear clear, honest feedback.

Building relational trust in your organization means prioritizing the creation of interpersonal relationships that are trusting, so that you have your ears and heart open to hear and see how you're showing up and what impact you may be having—despite your best intentions. Companies that have relational trust in place know how essential it is to mission success, because of its impact on interpersonal communication, productivity, and culture.

How can you create a safe space for conversations that foster relational trust? While relational trust doesn't demand friendship as a precursor, it certainly requires being authentically human with other humans. When an employee hits an emotional note, listen and ask open, honest questions. Find out what's important. The purpose of relational trust is to open the door—and the heart—for empathic presence with whoever in the organization has something to say. For the leader, this requires a stance that is other than dictatorial: it demands a willingness to hear what's being said, and a curiosity to double-click into conversations to really understand what's going on. It may be hard to hear. It may come as a surprise. You may want to shut it down. But instead, get curious about your reactions; what part of your shadow may you be glimpsing?

For any of us working within a dysfunctional organization where our point of view is not valued, heard, or seen, we may perceive ourselves as powerless. (Talk about tanking morale.) Think back to the last time you were shut down by someone in a perceived position of power. Whether it's our parents, our boss, or our investor, some part of us cringes if we feel someone is diminishing our existence as if we, or our points of view, don't matter. If we believe we are indeed powerless, we remain stuck to the fly tape of suffering in organizational misery.

To shift that state of powerlessness, ask yourself, How have I been complicit in creating the circumstances I say I want to change? Most often, we help create the conditions we don't want. Even in the most toxic work environment we have the opportunity to look closely at how we may be contributing to the situation. From there, you may be able to find a solid foothold in a new direction.

When we feel powerless, we often lose sight of how we can be our magnanimous self. When we act or react from that place of feeling small, we may do something we regret. Locating your most generous self allows you to show up in ways that are bigger than your small, scared, and likely defensive self. Even though that powerless-feeling part of you may be very alive, what inner move can you make to show up more magnanimously? How can you show up so you have no regrets?

Sharing the Load: Speaking in Confidence

We all have a need to be real and honest. We have a need to be heard and seen for the fullness of who we are and what's happening in our lives. And what's more, we all have a need to have our feelings and know it's okay to have them.

Reaching out to share our most vulnerable truth is challenging for reasons as varied as each of us are. When it comes to sharing what's in our hearts, not every audience is able to hear what's really going on for us. Sometimes when we do open up, the person we open up to isn't meeting our need to be heard and seen. Real listening is a hard job that not many people in our lives are particularly good at all the time.

What stops us from showing up as our honest truth? What does it take to feel safe and loveable, and perhaps find belonging by being all that we are, as we are? Such ideas can be new to many a nervous system that's not had that experience in spades. But if we can't be true to how we really feel, without parsing that out to an audience or trying to make someone else feel okay, we only enhance our isolation. As adults, what are the resources we can pull in or remember that help us feel safe and secure enough to say what we need to say in full confidence?

And on the flip side, what stops us from being the kind of person someone can come to in full confidence to share what's closest to their heart?

RED-YELLOW-GREEN

*The emotional brain responds to an event more
quickly than the thinking brain.*

—Daniel Goleman

Our weekly partners call at Reboot begins with a subversively
simple check-in: How are you? It's a line I've heard asked of different
audiences—from our four-person partners team to a workshop
filled with people—that somehow renders the person responding
to deliver a register of what's on their mind-heart-body, sometimes
bringing tears along with it.

How are you?—such a simple question, right? We call it Jerry's
big, hard question. Yet when asked as an offering, an invitation, to
show up with all of you in the safety of listening peers at the start of
a meeting, you begin with an authentic human connection which
becomes the point of departure for the agenda and tasks at hand.
This alone can bring profound shifts in how ideas flow and, later,
how the work gets done. The opportunity that lies in asking this
question, and listening to the response, is to tune in to what your
peers are feeling. To tune in to what *you* are feeling.

As each person responds, how we're doing on the inside gets
named and finds its place at the table, versus being an unnamed,
self-contained state deemed less important than the practical
matters at hand. When we sit with our unnamed inner states among
others in a meeting, those inner states can be misread by the group

as feelings that relate to the meeting matters at hand—not to what's inside us. Someone feels angry. One person is anxious because of a debacle on the home front. Another is worried about picking his daughter up after school with the project deadline looming overhead. Moreover, some folks' reactions to items on the agenda may seem over the top, or muted, or listless. You may find yourself in this situation becoming agitated or anxious by the tone, tenor, or demeanor of discussions. If you're like most humans, you may start making up heavily storied interpretations of what's happening, or decide that you are somehow the cause of all of this. That feeling and any trailing storylines may leave with you, post-meeting, and seep into the rest of your day's interactions.

I've worked in organizations where the feelings of leadership rippled through the whole team like sound waves. If the CEO was happy, there was a light-hearted feeling in the office. If it was a terse and anxious day, you could almost cut the tension in the air with a knife. Of course, no one on the leadership team said what was going on or what had them in such a state. Yet everyone else was reacting in their own way to the tension of unspoken—but felt—emotions.

What we're experiencing here can be described as emotional Wi-Fi. Psychologist and author Daniel Goleman explains emotional Wi-Fi as something that we're wired for deep in our neurology, thanks to mirror neurons—the parts of our wiring that help us sense our environment, learn, and connect with others. In a *New York Times* article titled "Friends for Life: An Emerging Biology of Emotional Healing," he writes:

> Mirror neurons are a widely dispersed class of brain cells that operate like neural Wi-Fi. Mirror neurons track the emotional flow, movement and even intentions of the person we are with, and replicate this sensed state in our own brain by stirring in our brain the same areas active in the other person. They enable extremely rapid synchronization

of people's posture, vocal pacing, and movements as they interact. In short, these brain cells seem to allow the interpersonal orchestration of shifts in physiology.

What Goleman is talking about can be simply stated as, "I feel you," as in, "I am feeling you in your state, and feeling my reaction as a reverberation of that." Mirror neurons are part of the same physiology that gets schools of fish to move together, birds to flock in complex murmurations, and horses to read their herd mates and the environment around them.

This is what helps us learn by watching others—from learning a new skill or sport to whatever we picked up around the dinner table growing up. Mirror neurons allow us to feel all the feels in movies as actors play out the unfolding plot. They help us tune in to things outside of us, such as the people in our lives, and are essential to being aware, empathic, and compassionate.

Emotional Wi-Fi is something we work with all the time as coaches. In coaching sessions, we can begin to feel any number of feelings from the client, such as angry or insecure. Or we start feeling like an imposter, which may be contrary to anything else in our way of being in the world at that moment in time. Yet a well-honed coach with ample self-awareness can discern that those strange feelings are what the client is feeling, even though the client hasn't named them yet. Good coaches use that information to help the client name what may be going on. Good leaders can do this as well.

One moment you can feel what you are feeling, and after a conversation or interaction or just being with another person, sans words, you may be able to pick up on a wholly other feeling. If you were happy before this interaction and suddenly began to feel, say, anger (yet have no reason in your world to feel that emotion), that's something to notice. You could very well be feeling what the other person is feeling; although depending on how deep the emotion is, they may not even be aware that they are feeling that emotion or be able to name it. This happens all the time in our work and home worlds, but how often do we realize that what we are feeling isn't necessarily ours?

Looking back to some of the more tense office environments I've worked in, I think about how things would have been different if leadership had said, "I'm stressed about finances and fundraising isn't going well," or "My toddler isn't sleeping through the night. I'm exhausted and feel like I'm failing," or whatever the case was. That simple reveal could have deflated a whole bunch of feelings rippling through the company (and the thoughts that come after those feelings), in as many varied ways as there are employees. There would have been relief that it was named, and very likely, empathy and compassion for what that person was going through. (Insert exhale here.)

We are all wired to read our environment as part of self-preservation. Studies have shown that only 7 percent of communication is verbal. That leaves us to differentiate the other 93 percent that is nonverbal: 55 percent through body language and 38 percent through tone of voice. As a result, we are constantly reading signs and cues from our fellow humans and interpreting those expressions through our own internalized "body language and tone of voice" dictionary. There's plenty of room for assumptive error there, as the universal look and sound of certain emotional states is a highly generalized thing. One person's expression for surprise could look like an expression of anger to someone else. Additionally, neurodiversity has taught us that some people have difficulty reading nonverbal cues at all.

At any company, whether you have authenticity neatly designed and displayed on your walls as value statements or not, there are feelings afoot. We are human organizations, after all, coming together to do great work and further our visions, all in the name of a greater purpose. Oftentimes the fundamental unit of doing that great work is a conversation. Conversations happen more easily, clearly, and harmoniously if we can connect as human beings, look each other in the eye, trust, and feel safe naming our inner state.

The beauty of naming your inner state is that you don't have to do anything with it. You just have to account for it and include it in your experience—versus pushing the feelings away. One of the mindfulness practices to help with this is what we at Reboot call Red–Yellow–Green. Based on Stephen Porges's polyvagal theory, which works with the different parts of the nervous system in our regulation or dysregulation, Red–Yellow–Green gives us a simple framework and common language. It works like this:

> Each group member does a quick check in on how they are doing—red, yellow, or green—and how they're entering the meeting. People may choose to share a bit more about what's behind their color choice, or perhaps a brief update about their life, work, or learning goal for the session. But long processing of these responses is not necessary and by no means required.

The basic rubric for these inner-state color markers is as follows:

> **Green** means you feel safe or are in flow. You're able to have eye contact, creativity, play, humor. In a sense, all systems are go.
>
> **Yellow** is reactionary, meaning that the fight-or-flight impulse is present, as is perhaps some defensiveness.
>
> **Red** means your rational brain is offline, nervous system is shutting down such that you may or may not be present at all, or there may be a loss of trust.

With this basic framing of the spectrum of our nervous system, consider these questions:

> What are some triggers that send you into the red? (They can be general, such as conflict, or very specific.)

> What does your body feel like when you are in the yellow?

> What are the signals or signs?

> What should others know about you when you are in the yellow or red?

> How can they help?

> What makes things worse?

> What type of contact do you need or not need?

The sea change of emotions that can grace our bodies on any given day, moment to moment, can be subtle or extreme. What we do with these emotions can give us insight and information, and help us work better and connect with other humans in our sphere.

The Red–Yellow–Green model shifts the tone of how you relate to folks and hold meetings. Being able to name your own inner state, or hear yourself name where you are, in a group check-in can have remarkable effects on how present you can be for yourself and others in the meeting. Listening to where others are in their inner states not only helps our nervous systems relax, it fosters a much greater sense of connection among the humans in the room (or virtual room).

As people begin to take their seat as leaders, they begin to discover that a big part of leadership is coaching. Tuning in to how *you* are is the first step to being present for all that arises in a day's work. And it can create a generative murmuration throughout your organization.

THE BIG REVEAL

The highest form of love is the love that allows for intimacy without the annihilation of difference.

—Parker J. Palmer

One evening I was walking my horse along the bridle paths towards the barn. The heat of the day had cooled off in the breeze rushing in over the ridgelines we could see in the distance. We walked side by side. Shoulder to shoulder. Occasionally stopping for a bite of grass, or pausing to take in the view. We were at ease and present with each other.

For me, the art of horsemanship is the art of partnership. The container of the relationship with each horse grounds me every day. It's a practice that makes me a better member of the herd as well as a better human with my human compadres. From what I've gathered thus far in my immersive study of all things horse, mastery in the realm of partnership involves being present for and with each other, and a big part of getting there is letting go of the stories I tell myself about what this relationship is, who my partner is, and how this is all going to work.

As one of my favorite horsemen, Andres Castano, notes: "When you stop controlling, you start communicating." Yet how do our ways of interacting or being in relationship keep us from real communication? How can we see things as they are instead of reacting to things based on expectation from past experiences? How can our interactions feel more like a dance, where we reach out for each other from the center of ourselves, moving along together with a sensibility of feel and the fullness of who we are intact?

Humans are story-making machines. Our imagination can serve us well and support our healing and transformation. Or it can help us weave tales that confirm our biases, our worst suspicions, and our most negative theories about ourselves, the situation, and the world at large. The story we tell ourselves usually has less to do with what's really happening and tends to be something we make out to be entirely about us. Most often, those stories don't end well in our imaginative projection screens, and we then operate as if these phantasmagorias are at play in real life. We react and respond from the story in our minds versus the reality of what's in front of us. In relationships, there's another human in front of us who may or may not be running versions of their own story while we're running ours. Whew! It's a miracle we get anything done together.

When it comes to relationships, it takes a lot of diligence for us to show up for each other on the neutral ground of reality. By *neutral* I'm referring to a place like Switzerland, where we arrive having laid down any arms and armor at the door. Or if we haven't unloaded such protective things before we enter, we at least know what we're carrying into the space of relating. How can we meet on the ground of reality, so that in that common space we can move forward together in clarity and grace?

If I'm running a storyline, it may contain names and characters from the current reality, but the meaning and feelings wrapped up in those tales say more about me—my projections and fears—than the reality of the person or situation in front of me. (This is a good thing to remind yourself of, especially as you listen to yourself reveal your machinations or if you are listening while someone reveals theirs.) These stories bear meanings that create more emotions and thoughts, which can trap us. Such tangled webs we can weave! These storylines are laced with our deepest fears. And when the scripts are writ large in our minds, we respond as if an act of self-preservation, with all the defenses we have in our arsenal. All these tactics usually take the other person in front of us as collateral damage.

But if we listen closely to these tales and inquire about them in a safe space, we can lift up and sift out what those very real fears are, what the emotions we're having might be telling us, and what's driving us in this moment and preventing us from actually connecting. Most often, airing the storylines in a safe space clears the air for everyone, especially in our most important relationships at home, work, and in the world.

The stories we tell ourselves must be handled with care. We must become aware of them, contain them in a narrative, and put them in quarantine for further inquiry and appreciation. If we decide to share, we need to place them upon the ground of reality where we can then meet each one with compassion.

A client of mine once shared how she really felt about a person with whom she was close in her life. She articulated the feelings and we identified the stories she was making up and the fears she had. I asked her if she would ever reveal that to the person by saying, "I'm feeling _____. The story I'm telling myself is _____. I'm afraid that _____."

She looked at me like I was entirely nuts and exclaimed, "No way! I could never let him know that!"

"Then how will he know where you really are?" I countered.

I refer to those moments in which we share what's going on for us—and what stories we are telling ourselves about the other person or situation, or the rest of what's captured in our mythmaking—as big reveals. A big reveal can feel like a big deal, but it's a proactive way to relate on the ground of reality with another being. Having the big reveal in your toolbox is a way to come back to the here and now, in the presence of another. Without it, you may not really be relating from a place of presence at all.

The art of partnership is learning where you are and where your partner is, and relating to each other from a place of reality versus the mythmaking theaters of our minds (where we enter relationship from a place of projection, fear, acting out, active or passive aggression, asserting power over, and other forms of story-making). Partnership is learning the art of being together in full-bodied presence and feeling what's emerging at the interplay of the space between us.

That is not an enmeshed sentiment in which each individual in the relationship fuses with the other. A healthy model of relationship holds the relationship we have with ourselves front and center, as a prerequisite. The space you hold for yourself as you are in relationship to another—in work, in intimacy, in family life—is a space that's wholly yours. After all, it is *your* life that is lived out in your body.

I look to how horses operate within the herd for a great example of being together without losing yourself. Horses, with their horizontally oriented bodies, relate to each other in bubbles of space. They feel the best knowing and clarifying two points in space:

a) I'm here, and

b) You're there.

Individually they are complete circles that maintain their space for the safety of each other and that of the herd. Once the edges of their personal space bubbles are established, they can decide to move together or not. The stronger the individual boundary, the more each horse knows how to connect with the other, and a stronger bond can form. The horse's nervous system can then relax. That clarity gives them a deep sense of psychological safety (an important catchphrase in conversations on work culture these days). In this way, how horses show up in the world lives out a riff from Brené Brown in that when it comes to boundaries, clarity is kindness.

This boundary setting can seem counterintuitive to many humans, namely because we perceive boundaries as points of disconnection rather than ways to find connection. Yet the best relationships are those with boundaries that are not only intact but are maintained through the sanctity of them. Two whole individuals, each on their own feet. Neither entity is lost in the other. They are not collapsed, divided, or subtracted.

> What makes you collapse yourself in order to be in relationship?

> Where does that show up in your leadership?

> What about yourself do you often give up?

> What part of you says you can't be fully yourself and be safe, or loved, or find belonging, in relationship with each other?

> Where do you lose yourself in relation to others at home, work, and in life?

In his book *Passionate Marriage: Keeping Love and Intimacy Alive in Committed Relationships*, relationship therapist David Schnarch notes that differentiation in relationship means standing on your own two feet so solidly that reaching out to the other is a choice from that place of fullness. We have to belong to ourselves first, before we can make that reach. "While differentiation allows us to set ourselves apart from others and determines how far apart we sit," he writes, "it also opens the space for true togetherness. It's about getting closer and more distinct, rather than more distant."

Yet so few of us actually know where we are. We become fused to many things in life, not just the people in our herd; our way of being can become so dependent on whatever we are hooked on emotionally and mentally that our very physiology, reactions, or level of shutdown can be contorted. To reveal what's truly happening for us in the theater of our minds (which is a big part of our human experience)—to ourselves *and* the person we are with—is a big moment of reckoning. Once we take our very self into account, we become internally located again to find our own two feet.

As mentioned in the essay "Red–Yellow–Green" on page 240, one of the tools we at Reboot use internally and with every client team is this set of questions:

> ➤ How am I?
>
> ➤ What is my body doing?
>
> ➤ What are my thoughts doing?
>
> ➤ What emotions am I having?
>
> ➤ What do I need right now?
>
> ➤ Where am I in relation to this present moment?

When each of us at the table or in the circle is given the time and space to check in about where we're at, the feeling tone of the meeting changes before it even really starts. It's as if we all arrive at the present and feel safer about being together. What we discover from each other is a sense of "Here I am. And I know where you are too."

All too often, we rush over from our "circle of space" (borrowing an image from the horses) to fix, save, advise, or somehow make the other person better. In doing so, we lose our own sense of self as we find ourselves in their circle of space, not our own.

Checking in with yourself first is a form of self-responsibility and self-care. In practice, this is one way to begin breaking habits and expectations in relationships by staying connected to where you are right now, how much energy you have, what you need, and what you're available for. It's also a great practice to establish or reestablish where you are in relation to feeling your feet firmly on the ground versus getting caught up in the circle of space that the other person is in. Finding this ground sets a clear note for yourself: This is where I end. Over there is where you begin. We are not one thing; we are two things in relation to one another.

To be self-responsible in relationship is all about clear boundaries. As my therapist wisely says, "Sovereignty is potent."

When we have established that place for ourselves, we can then be curious about what's happening in the world of experience for the other person, in hopes that we can meet or connect and possibly converse on the grounds of reality. We inquire, "Where are you, over there, where you begin at the edges of your meatsuit? I'm curious what's happening in your worldview." In doing so, we trust that they are on their own space around their own self-responsibility (a big assumption, knowing how hard it can be for *us* to find our own feet; but leave that responsibility with them in their circle.).

Here's an example. A simple exchange between two people could look like this:

Me: [internally checking in] How am I right now? How available am I?

Me: [checking in with you] "How are you? I am here with little energy, but is there something I can do for you?"

You: "[Make request]"

Me: "I can do ten minutes and be more available tomorrow. Is that okay?"

What transpires from this stance is a gentle negotiation and assertion of space that's based on where you are right now, what you're coming in with, and what you've got to give. It's a way to name the stories you're telling yourself about what may or may not be really happening. It's a stance that's clear and relieving. That sovereignty *is* potent. Clarity is kindness, after all. This way of relating can feel so radically different than anything we've done, felt, or seen modeled previously in our lives. What a difference it can make in the quality of the space between us and what we can accomplish.

When it comes to leading together, working together, partnering in life, parenting together, and being in community together, these skills are paramount to successful relating and the getting-done of things. Standing where we are on our own two feet and taking self-responsibility is the first step to leading shoulder to shoulder and achieving great things together.

Part VI

EMBODIED
LEADERSHIP

BODYFULNESS AND WISE ACTION

In leadership and in life, the body is a source of knowing and doing. Failing to include the body in our experience of leadership makes for a disembodied leadership. It's hard to be fully present when you're disassociated, and it's hard to connect to others and your life when you're *here* only from the neck up. Humane leadership is rooted in the fullness of being human. Yet being at home and fully alive in our meatsuit can be challenging for many of us. No one gives us operating instructions for being human when we land here, and we're left to figure it out from the environments that raised us. We can shift much of that patterning of responses and way of being in our body in the world by practicing something more inclusive than mindfulness: bodyfulness.

Coming home to our body is no small task. To be a fully alive leader, one who practices bodyfulness, means being present to feel things within yourself and from the world around you, and then act from that place with wisdom and intention.

There are no easy, one-size-fits-all answers to the following questions, but asking them is the first step in finding your path to become such a leader:

> ➤ How do you access the knowledge of being in your body?
> ➤ How do you learn to tune in to the various levels of awareness you have within yourself about you and your surroundings?

> How do you learn about and harvest the information in your emotions?

> How do you regulate your nervous system so that you can take care of your side of the street before you show up for and with others?

> What traumas are held in your body that show up in your relationships, and what steps do you take towards healing them?

> How do you remain in connection with your body through big decisions, hard conversations, and moments when your amygdala is hijacked?

> How do you honor what's true for you? What is a full-bodied yes when making commitments and defining boundaries of what is and is not okay?

> How do you stay embodied with your colleagues, family, partner, co-founders, and investors?

WHOLENESS AND LEADERSHIP

I do not want to be complicit in wiping myself out, and denying myself as a whole, broken-hearted, messy, human being.

—Jerry Colonna

Our friend Parker Palmer writes, "Wholeness does not mean perfection; it means embracing brokenness as an integral part of life." Embracing our humanity—the fact that we're human, not perfect automatons—is a liberating realization for our hearts. Doing so consciously allows us perhaps, for once, to be fully ourselves—shamelessly.

Showing up in our fullness means embracing all that's in our lives: what's happened to us in the past and what's happening now that we'd rather ignore. It means embracing all the parts of us with a sense of compassion, and becoming an adult with all our feelings and complexes and wounds from past baggage sorted out. It means we have to slow down a bit to let it all in, include messy parts we've kept tucked away, examine our habits and how we live our lives, and decide what kind of adult we want to be. It means we must trust the process to understand ourselves fully so we can transform our lives into authentic expressions of who we really are. We then can abandon our attempts to fit our very intricate selves into preformatted containers offered by the world with their defined perfection that would level us in the pursuit.

Sometimes I bring clients into a different arena for coaching sessions. We spend our time together accompanied by my horse in a dirt coral with a beautiful view of the Continental Divide, a pair of eagles nesting nearby, and hawks, coyotes, and other ground critters occasionally coming to visit. Each session has its own lesson plan, and yet there's a key element that seems to happen each time: clients get a sense of who they really are and their innate way of being—without the personas, coping mechanisms, defenses, and fears.

When clients touch on that sense of being, when they articulate it for themselves, or when they feel it light up in the neural networks of their bodies again, it usually brings a tender moment and perhaps some tears of recognition. One client asked, "Why is it so hard to be this way in the world? Why does it feel so risky to be me?"

Why does it feel so risky to be me? That question reverberates in me. Our early experiences cause us to put the damper on our brightest self. Sometimes I liken the image of us surviving our childhood with our precious self intact to a quarterback running down the field protecting the ball, trying not to be tackled by the defense. Many times, in our present, we're still crouched around the ball so that no one takes it (us) away from us. The imprints from our past linger so strongly and if left unchecked will rule our current state of being, never allowing us to feel safe enough to relax and let ourselves feel *free*.

Embracing our wholeness means looking closely and compassionately at all the parts and pieces of ourselves—the wounds and all that survived—and finding the beauty in what may feel like a broken inner world. It means being real about that big art project of wholeness that we are and bring with us in our work, families, friendships, partnerships, and the deepest relationship we have: the one with ourselves and our own inner landscape. Somewhere in that process, we can find love again and choose to move forward rather than remain contracted by fear.

Here at Reboot, we often say that "better humans make better leaders." Though in reality, better humans also make for better mothers, fathers, partners, friends, neighbors, and policymakers. Becoming a better human requires a deep self-inquiry that can begin for you with these questions:

> When you look in the mirror, who do you see?

> Who in your life helps you see both your truth and what holds you back?

> What are demons that lie at the heart of your human experience? What don't you want to see about yourself?

> How are you complicit in creating what you say you don't want?

> How can you bring more compassion to yourself?

> What helps your resiliency?

Then as leaders, we must ask ourselves:

> What might happen if we attempted to lead from a place of honesty, equanimity, and compassion?

> How might we transform our organizations and workplaces into safe oases where our fullest selves emerge, allowing us to step into purpose and the meaningful work of our lives—and allow those who work with us to do the same?

THE PERPETUAL UNDOING

Helping, fixing, and serving represent three different ways of seeing life. When you help, you see life as weak. When you fix, you see life as broken. When you serve, you see life as whole. Fixing and helping may be the work of the ego, and service the work of the soul.

—Rachel Naomi Remen

As I learned to conquer my fears by taking a leap of faith and breathing into the unknown, I thought it was the best thing ever and everyone should do it too. I wanted everyone to harness their creativity and break free from the boxes and chains that keep them contained. At the time, discoveries like that felt wholly novel to me. I couldn't wait to share them. But from the outside, I'm sure it looked like I thought I was reinventing personal growth.

When I first started out on the course to being a "helper person" (what a friend of mine called the coach, counselor, consultant-type), I thought I had at least some very key things about the world, figured out. I'd try to offer up the latest learnings, but that wasn't always what my semi-captive audience members needed. With a limited toolbox in tow, I learned that helping people change required more than advice on how to do this "just leap and breathe into the fear" thing. Such distilled methodology and cookie cutter solutions aren't a custom fit. I couldn't help my people from that place, nor could I fix them.

Part of me believed I could, and I focused on being of value in that way. Instead of fixing them, however, I was discounting their experience, since whatever desire I had to help was really more about me. It wasn't until I learned that an agenda-free, openhearted, unassuming presence alone was the most useful stance in meeting people where they are.

This stance of being of service, versus thinking I had the answers to bestow upon others, took inner work culminating in the perpetual undoing of my identity. Just when I thought I knew who I was and how the world worked, the model shifted. In the process, I was skillfully erased over and over again. The helper-fixit ego checked. My book of answers turned to questions in the face of the ever-mutating truth of both me and the world around me.

When we get stuck and attached to our identities, we begin to assume that we are a static, fixed self, and blatantly deny life's current of mutability. Constant change is the only constant, and our very sense of self is a fluid unit.

Reverend angel Kyodo williams, in a September 2020 conversation with Krista Tippett on the "On Being" podcast, refers to this discomfort as "uncomfortably unknowing ourselves." It is the "willingness to keep being willing to come undone—to do what we can to understand the world around us and how we operate, what is impacting who we are and how we are, and to allow that to keep coming undone."

The edge of who we think we are is an interesting place. It's the boundary between known, unknown—including the ignored, denied parts of us—and unknowing the constructed faces, personas, and dogmatic beliefs. Some folks have edges they defend because their ego depends on it. I'm sure we have all encountered at least a few of these folks and perhaps can identify when we do the same to some degree. Others can reside in the space of undoing, putting who they think they are and what they know to the side, meeting life with curiosity.

"Awe is the moment when the ego surrenders to wonder," writes author and activist Terry Tempest Williams. Wonder and awe are moments of freedom—a supple place that leads to a pathway of resilience because we are present to what is. In a sense, there's less of a struggle there because our sense of self is not always at stake; our identities aren't rigid. If we can let go of our attachments to our role as a leader, or perhaps our over-identification with our company, we can arrive at a place where we can connect with those we're wanting to serve, and serve them better. A hard concept in practice, that suppleness.

When we focus our energies on upholding a certain identity anywhere in life, we can create a tension around the very image we cling to. When life happens in the random way that it does, part or parts of us can limit our capacity to deal with things with the clarity and grace of compassion.

This way of being in leadership isn't something you get from a how-to book. This is an embodied way of meeting life, the humans you encounter and collaborate with, and all the varied things that happen on any given day at work.

Our way of being affects our way of doing. It also affects those working alongside us towards the same vision, like our employees or our life partners. If we persist in operating in ways that are stressful and full of struggle—not scaling as a leader by managing all the decisions, not delegating, demonstrating poor communication and collaboration, lack of time management, in the weeds thinking, and failure to manage emotions—we'll find ourselves on the fast track to burnout, perhaps taking a few folks down with us along the way. The time comes when we need to explore a new frontier and a new way of meeting the very real challenges of leading and running organizations. That's when it's critical to ask:

> How am I creating this (panting, manic, insert your adjective of choice here) drive that keeps me going?

> What change am I trying to make in the world, and what changes do I need to make within me in how I approach this?

> What identity is tied up in this way of doing things?

Deep Listening

How we are in the world—our being—affects how we do things in the world—our doing—when it comes to our presence. With less stress and anxiety, our ways of being with each other can make work easier. We often talk about the Red–Yellow–Green check-ins as a human way to begin meetings. If you incorporate this practice, notice what happens for you as you do. Do you find that you want to interject? What is it that you want to say? How did what was said make you feel? Is what you want to say for the person who is speaking, or is it for you (and what you're feeling)?

If you're on the lookout for where your edges show up, notice what happens when you try to listen. I've experienced a great dearth in quality listening. When I don't feel heard, it often doesn't feel safe to speak, and that doesn't make for a two-way conversation (as mentioned earlier in the book, I call these "non-versations").

A good listener is an oasis where there's space to speak, where silence is welcomed, and there's a big ear witnessing it all through an empathetic and curious human. It's a space where I don't feel rushed to speak lest someone fill the space, where silence has a place, where I don't feel trampled by assertions, advising, attempts to fix because what I say makes the other anxious (or a ream of possible feelings that arise).

I encourage you to try this exercise at work or at home:

Set aside five minutes with someone. One of you will be the listener, one of you will be the talker in round one (you'll switch in round two). Set a timer for two minutes. The talker talks for the full two minutes. Even if the talking stops before two minutes is up, let silence fill the space until the timer runs out. All the while, the listener simply listens (no talking!). After the first two minutes, switch roles and set the timer for another two minutes. After the final two-minute timer is up, share with each other what that experience was like for you as listener and talker.

Reflect on the following:

> How did that go?

> How was it to just listen? What did that feel like? What came up for you?

> How was it to be heard? What did that feel like?

> What did you learn about yourself in this exercise?

WORKING WELL

*A business leader's job is to create great teams
that do amazing work on time.*

—Patty McCord

The majority of humans spend as much time at work (if not more) as they do on their mattress. Much like a bad mattress, a less-than-great work environment takes a toll on our vitality and can squash our joie de vivre. There was a statistic floating around our office for a while postulating that 70 percent of people are unhappy at work.[*] Showing up day after day for something that fails to ignite your inner fire takes a toll on your mental and physical health. What kind of work can a company produce when human hearts at the helm are all in malaise? The antidote can be found at the core of our humanity.

We've all seen or been on the receiving end of someone not stoked about their job, and perhaps we've been there ourselves. It's a crappy-feeling place to be. Perhaps we've watched our parents endure work in this way, and we've set out to do something different, yet perhaps find ourselves in a similar place (even though we may be at a glossy startup with free lunch).

Work-related stress comes in many forms, most of which are due to the interpersonal environments in which we work and how

---

[*] This figure, from a 2013 "Gallup State of the Workplace Report," was cited by many news outlets.

that affects our intrapersonal environment. When we encounter delusional thinking, lack of clarity, and lack of radical honesty in any area of our life, it rattles our trust. At the core of our neurology, we don't feel safe. And when we don't feel safe, we're typically running on fight-or-flight (fear)—a draining state to be in continuously. At work, that can be amplified with additional feelings of imposter syndrome, inadequacy, and self-doubt. Our sense of belonging may feel threatened.

Those few things alone will make anyone want to curl into a ball and hide—not be the productive, positive, strategic people employers would like on their team. What's more, all that stress spins in wasted cycles of human energy, which means doing less, even less efficiently: from missed deadlines and products that don't ship to a hearty helping of team dysfunction.

This level of emotional work stress takes a toll on employees as well as the product, brand, and execution of the larger vision of your organization (which may then stress out your VCs). To put some light metrics on this: eight hours of wasted human productivity times the number of people in your organization equals a lot of wasted hours of productivity.

Yikes.

While work doesn't have to be this way, this begs the question: What does it take to build resilient and humane organizations? To unearth the answer when working with clients, we often begin by asking, "What kind of company do *you* want to work for?" It's a big question, because it truly does begin with *you*.

You have the responsibility and the audacious capacity to create that kind of organization every single day. And more self-inquiry, with the following questions, will help you discover how:

> What kind of culture are you creating now?

> Are you creating one of tension born of dysfunction?

> Are you creating one that promotes ways of being that lead to burnout?

> Are you creating one of safety and belonging so that people succeed?

Humans need to feel safe, to feel a sense of belonging, and to feel loved. These elements, when tended to, create environments for the fight-or-flight parts of us to shift into less stress and more of the good work we all long for as employees and employers. By honoring this basic, subtle, and important part of our shared humanity, we build work environments that can handle the roller coaster of highs and lows that come with fast growth of a scaling organization—or one of any size and stature.

Consider that company values and culture are the ways in which an organization operates, moment to moment, and ask yourself:

> What are the values you live by in the office?

> What does your organization feel like?

> How are tough conversations handled (or are they)?

> How is emotional intelligence fostered companywide?

> How are decisions made?

> How does the company listen?

> How does the company collaborate?

> How does the company give and receive feedback?

> Is everyone clear about their roles and responsibilities and reporting structures?

> How is vision communicated? Is it well understood?

> Does everyone have what they need to succeed?

The interpersonal spaces that create our workplaces are like the spaces between the atoms that create our solid world. It's those spaces that matter and make a difference in how we operate and what we build. When we take care of what's happening in our intrapersonal space as leaders, managers, business owners, and employees, our interpersonal spaces stand a better chance of improving. As Parker Palmer says: "If you choose to live an unexamined life, please don't take a job that involves other people."

We started Reboot because we believe that the possibility of fully realizing our human potential lies in our work. Work doesn't have to destroy us. Work can be the way in which we achieve our fullest selves. It's a movement around how we work and how we can work differently. Building humane workplaces is the best place to begin.

SPIRITUAL CRISIS, SPIRITUAL OPPORTUNITY

You have the need and the right to spend part of your life caring for your soul. It is not easy. You have to resist the demands of the work-oriented, often defensive, element in your psyche that measures life only in terms of output—how much you produce—not in terms of the quality of your life experiences. To be a soulful person means to go against all the pervasive, prove-yourself values of our culture and instead treasure what is unique and internal and valuable in yourself and your own personal evolution.

—Jean Shinoda Bolen

The body has a way of letting us know when we need to slow down. Yet how well do we listen? Blowing past the sensations and signals typically results in the body getting loud and clear with us about when it's time to be still and listen. The body will try to get our attention until we heed the call to care for our soul. Then we can begin striding in tune with our personal evolution—led by what's calling us to and guiding us from a deeper part of our inner life.

When the soul comes knocking, we often know it in our body. It shows up as increased anxiety, tension, symptoms, and ailments of various kinds, and a series of unfortunate events may seem to find us like a plague. Unresolved issues, pent-up or buried emotions, or things that need to be said (e.g., boundaries that have been crossed but not acknowledged) will surface as stress. This stress shows up in our body, somewhere or another. It's as if the soul cries out through our very flesh and blood and bones, begging us to turn towards ourselves in a way we haven't before so that we can dip below the superficial layer of life we've known. (At one point in my life when I knew I needed to leave a relationship, all the stress of unspoken feelings and pent-up stress of not saying what I needed to say showed up as a full-body rash. It was the middle of winter and a co-worker saw it peeking out of my sleeve and asked if I had a really bad sunburn.)

The long string of unfortunate events—physical or otherwise—set us back from something, some place, some destination we had in mind, and render us unable to move with the same getting-through-it-ness techniques that worked up until they didn't anymore.

Sometimes, until we hit a rock bottom, all of this feels easy to blip over in pursuit of other things. For example, how often do we power through an impending cold, coffee and cough suppressants in hand, to keep on keepin' on with the inbox, in the meetings, in the airports—like we're running on all cylinders? Who clears their calendar for a day to rest and let the body do what it needs to heal?

Even if we get the message to slow down, what are we listening for, exactly? What's happening where soul meets body, where spirit meets bone? Sometimes the messages are abundantly clear; other times you have to look askew to catch a fleeting glimpse or rely on other ways of knowing in order to fully understand. Sometimes you have to drop your old maps and dictionaries, and other learned ways of knowing, and surrender to the knowing that stirs in the deeper dimension—larger than just our rationales and cellularly rooted part—of our whole being.

In the midst of an unexplainable onslaught of aches and pains and unrelenting rashes, we may find ourselves in what psychologist Nicole LePera calls "a spiritual crisis." She notes that at rock bottom—whether physical, emotional, mental, or all the above—is a pull to heal. Here we can open up to the latent wisdom within us and dig deep into some self-healing. We can track our wily ego, converse with our future self, reparent our inner child, learn what we really want, and set our intentions accordingly. We can learn about our emotional addictions, detox our bodies, get clear about our boundaries, and feel what's behind our anxieties. We grow up, and grow ourselves. We learn the art of self-care and to shut the door on the outside world. In that way we can nurture and incubate our inner creative storehouse of lifeforce, curiosity, and fierce and tender love for our very self.

The life the soul holds for us and the life that awaits us may look radically different from the ambitions we've initially been eager to follow. Often that life of the soul isn't borne of the same sentiments we have for our ambitions: the part of us that wants to do, achieve, and make something of ourselves is often fueled by unconscious drivers. None are bad or incorrect, as they got us this far. However, they may not be effective strategies for moving forward as they likely lack a holistic vision of who we are in our entirety and what future life is flowing in and calling us to do.

Once you arrive here, there's no figurin' this out in the ways you're used to. There are no hacks. You must open the door to the place you've shoved unresolved feelings, family loyalties, past hurts, and fears. You must choose self-care and self-healing over outwardly striving towards goals set by an external locus, or the need to please or belong to something or someone other than yourself.

But the good news is: you've arrived. The soul has come knocking to show you another way of meeting life—one where you are not merely fitting in but belong in your wholeness.

When we experience the limitations of our old well-worn strategies, we can assume a new identity with which to move through life—a more whole version of ourselves. And we can let our lives— and our leadership—speak from there.

THE SECRETS OF A SUCCESSFUL ENTREPRENEUR

To dwell in the here and now does not mean you never
think about the past or responsibly plan for the future.
The idea is simply not to allow yourself to get lost in
regrets about the past or worries about the future.

—Thich Nhat Hanh

When we face the unknowns ahead of us, fear can creep up to the forefront of our experience and direct our imagination into the realm of anxieties. As entrepreneurs, we know this grab bag of anxieties all too well: the restlessness, working long hours to stay ahead of things, sleepless nights, and feeling like we don't know and can't learn fast enough to avoid potential failure (as if knowledge in and of itself really protects us). It's hard to know which way to go, what to say, or who to listen to. Knowing where you are, and having a clear connection to all the knowing available to you when you're calm, can give you the clarity you need to navigate from that expansive place rather than be contracted by fear.

Sometimes it feels like the regrets of the past and the anxieties of the future pull at us with shoulds. This can happen in a myriad of ways. Some of us fall prey to imposter syndrome at this juncture. Sometimes, we simply have a hard time knowing which way to go, perhaps not being sure how to appease the tug and pull of our obligations and guilt.

Fear can prevent us from being our fullest selves, like when we get caught up mitigating things that haven't happened yet, in response to things we haven't even done yet: "If I do X, then someone will do Y. Therefore, I can't do X. But I want to do X. But what if doing that thing backfires in some way?" When I begin managing the perceived possibility of someone else's reaction to something I've done, did, or want to do, I know my past is showing up in my present and I'm not really grounded in reality. The tangle of that web of anxiety feels like the fly tape that holds me stuck in the fear of losing a sense of safety, love, and belonging from someone/something. In moments like that, my clarity of self, sovereignty, intention, and action is obfuscated by my fears about what other people will say or do to me if I do the thing I want to do—or even if I just be who I am.

In that move, the proverbial *they* have all the power over me. When I give up my power in this way, I abandon myself. Fear overrides my agency and my own two feet on the ground. I forget that power was mine in the first place.

We can give up our power in as many ways as we let fear drive us. The good news is we can take it back whenever we'd like.

If only we could get it right, we think, maybe we'll be bulletproof and won't feel the sting of our stronger emotions when they arise—or feel so paralyzed by them. Perhaps we'll be impervious and not feel the turbulence of intense emotions at all.

Would we be able to get it right if we mastered our day-to-day living such that we could do everything in a day to keep ourselves together: work out, meditate, eat well, work with a sense of purpose, be a good parent and partner and lover, save for retirement, floss, stretch, journal, and drink enough water? It's hard to have our sh*t together if we are being measured by all the criteria of the world out there. It's easy to feel like we're flailing and failing if we rail against that bar of perceived superhuman excellence.

We do want our best life and (hopefully) want to be the best human we can be. The place we scramble and lose our foothold is when we give up the rating scale for our life to the outside world that's judging our worth by the likes, hearts, comments, reactions, and opinions of others. In that case, we can be ruled by the fear that without accolades, or not doing all the things superhumans do, we are nothing. We have not only given up our data to an algorithm (if you chart all of this on apps), but we've given our power over to someone else. And we suffer tremendously. We live stuck between the shoulds and the anxieties. Tugged and pulled, this way and that, and likely feeling a good dose of not good enough—or some flavor of shame—along the way.

The best and brightest among us (that's you!) know how to take this power back. We know we only momentarily *misplace* it from time to time. As my mom says to me in those moments when she hears me spinning in my own fear-driven thoughts, "Remember, Ali: The force is with you."

What part of us gets hooked on what the outside world thinks? Our wily ego worries about these things, as if our worth is in the hands of something outside of us.

And I am reminded of Lewis Carroll's *Through the Looking Glass* when Alice enters the Woods with No Name. She forgets her name and is guided by a deer, who also has no name. As the story goes:

So, they walked on together though the wood, Alice with her arms clasped lovingly round the soft neck of the Fawn, till they came out into another open field, and here the Fawn gave a sudden bound into the air and shook itself free from Alice's arms. "I'm a Fawn!" it cried out in a voice of delight, "and, dear me! you're a human child!" A sudden look of alarm came into its beautiful brown eyes, and in another moment it had darted away at full speed.

For a while, Alice and the fawn had a direct experience of non-ego. This is perhaps one of the most peaceful and loving scenes in either of the books detailing Alice's adventures in Wonderland. It also is one of the most peaceful and loving scenes we can arrive at for ourselves, as a sweet respite from the bizarre and frightening things we experience in our own mental wonderlands.

"What we wear without realizing it is the ego," writes Meggan Watterson, author of *Mary Magdalene Revealed*.

> It's the stories we've covered ourselves with or the stories we have used to obscure the truth of who we really are. And the ego is so well-meaning. It's like the helicopter mom who thinks we need protection and thinks fear will keep us safe. The ego builds up all these layers of why we should be afraid of who we are, or why we should feel shame about who we've been.

"Don't let the rules, projections, and expectations of a society that doesn't see your true image define you," Watterson cautions us. I'm not sure who else might find an exquisite leadership book inside this book about Mary Magdalene, but I sure did. While pouring over each page, it was clear to me that Mary Magdalene was perhaps the first executive coach. If she were still alive, I'd hire her at Reboot, stat.

Bear with me while I muse a bit: If Mary Magdalene was a present-day executive coach, she'd help us upgrade our egoic operating system to react differently. "How can you find yourself in the moments where you feel lost, alone, heartbroken, not sure what to do?" she'd ask. I imagine she'd write articles for *Wired* and *Inc.* titled "The Seven Secrets of a Successful Leader," and the enumerated points would sound something like these lines from Watterson's book:

1. Learn to see with the eye of the heart.

2. No one outside of you knows more than you do about *you*. You do not need to give away any of your power to anyone, ever.

3. Know your worth. Believe in yourself, in your own voice, in what you know is true, even if the world around you does not confirm this truth for you.

4. Move from power *over* to power *with*.

5. You can always begin again.

6. Doing your inner work is the key to freedom. The inner transformation creates the outer transformation.

7. Love yourself enough to ask for assistance.

Hers would be a master class on leadership that merges the ego and the soul to become more fully human. And it would directly apply to our entrepreneurial roller coaster rides—in fact, to life in general.

Watterson's message sounds subversively simple yet can serve as a solid guide to keep you upright and your integrity airtight, while moving through life's weather patterns and external noise. Watterson writes:

> Sometimes the most loving thing to do doesn't appear to be the bravest. It's not about pushing through or overpowering fear. Sometimes we just need to be with where we are terrified. And not ask the terror to leave or change. But dare to become the one who can hold it in a love that didn't exist before it, a love that grew, and expanded in order to meet it.

This is a great alternative to habits we may have that cause us to abandon ourselves and give away our power to the clamor of the world outside us. Instead, when we sit with our fears, hurts, confusions, and at-a-loss-ness, we can find a deeper power that is *with* us, not *over* us. We can meet ourselves in those moments, finding solace, and our own two feet, and a whole lot of love. It's like a balm for our worried and anxious selves as long as we remember that it's there, waiting for us.

The secret of a successful entrepreneur is in knowing this maneuver, and returning to it when needed. There is no place where we can be so smart as to evade all the feelings that life will evoke. There is no level of consciousness that will protect us from those feelings either. And no matter how much of your shadow you unpack, there will always be more. You can't evade (or take a pill for) your humanity.

Forgetting and returning to what we know, and who we are, is essential to the human experience, equal to experiencing the wide range of feelings (both pleasant and unpleasant) available to us. How we include the fullness of our humanity bolsters our wholeness (and, I'd argue, our connection to joy through it all).

"The choice we have, the opportunity that's presented to us in those moments of exquisite pain, is to also remember the soul," notes Watterson.

> "We can bring in the other half of what it means to be human. Not right away, or at least not at first. We can just let it sit on our shoulder or in our back pocket. And even that little presence of light might help us move through the pain differently than we had before... Try not to curse the pain, or avoid it. Or to feel like a failure because of it. Try not to run from it, and numb it. Try to see it as our chance to reach a love that can withstand it. Not permanently; nothing is permanent. Just in this moment. That's all that matters. Find the presence of love in those moments when before you had abandoned yourself."

Take a moment to ponder Watterson's words. And consider what it will take for *you* to achieve your own moment of stark reality, when you find yourself fully present in the moment and perfectly aligned with body and soul, by asking yourself:

> Underneath the ego and all the ways you get hooked on evaluating, judging, and rating yourself, who are you?

> Who are you under the layers of internalized messages from your culture, lineage, family system, early history, the roles you've assumed, the titles next to your name, and the outfits you don?

> What are the masks you wear to face the world? When you take them all off, what do you find?

> What commitments are you willing to make to listen to your own heart?

I hope you find the strength of *you*. The same fiery strength that allowed Joan of Arc to declare: "I am not afraid. I was born to do this." This strength comes from an integrity that is aligned first and foremost with your heart. It's as close as your breath (or maybe three deep ones).

SEEING HOW FAR
YOU'VE COME

Have you ever looked up and realized that where you are now is where you once wished you might be? It's a powerful moment. I've found that the time it takes to manifest what we'd hoped for can vary in delivery speed. Yet when our desire finally comes to fruition, a lot comes into perspective for us.

Taking time to reflect, at this point in your journey, can bring to the surface immense gratitude and appreciation for how things played out, and what is here for you *now*. Perhaps you'll even notice an appreciation for *who* you are now, as you consider the following:.

> - What's here for you now at this juncture?

> - What is your relationship to your current work? When would you know you were "done"?

> - What does success look like to you now?

> - How are you present, in this moment? What part of you wants to be someplace else?

> - Who was the version of you who once wanted to be where you are now? What was that version of you most concerned about?

> - What have you learned about yourself and the world since then? What is the current version of you most concerned about?

> What do you see now that you want to change? What would be different if things changed in that way? How would things feel?

> What is here, in your present moments, for you to enjoy, that you deserve? What is here to be grateful for? What is here to celebrate?

> Where do you find purpose? What do you love?

> How would you like to keep going from this place?

CONCLUSION: AT THE HEART OF IT ALL

Regardless of the myths we are telling ourselves, what kind of company or organization are we truly building? At the end of our days, are we becoming the person we'd like to be?

—Jerry Colonna

The art of leading well isn't learned from a playbook or gleaned from a checklist of things to do. Having frills in the office or Casual Fridays do not make a great culture. Yes, there are things a leader needs to do. But if you're not embodying the values behind the task, you'll miss the point. Leadership is a process of becoming, and as such, good leadership demands plenty of room for reflection.

Leadership happens when you step fully into yourself, claim who you are, and take your seat in your company (no matter what your role) and your life. It requires taking a fresh look at what's in front of you, free from your usual fears and clouding judgements. Leadership means taking hold of your birthright, your inherent wholeness. It's being fierce, wise, compassionate, and honest with yourself, and acting with integrity.

Knowing yourself enough to arrive at, return to, and resource yourself from the center of your being is at the heart of leading from love. Love is being present.

When it came to building our company, I sat in the tension between strategy and structure as COO. Part of my job was to plan the work and work the plan—to operate and execute towards where we said we were heading. The things I kept in the back of my mind that guided the to-do lists were qualitative questions: Are we executing according to our vision and mission? Are we in integrity? Are we clear about what we're creating, what needs to be done, and who's doing what?

The Big Question that hung right near our decision making and visioning was: Are we building the company we want to work for? And it has become our guiding principle in many decisions: how we define our benefits and company policies; how we want to interface with potential clients; how we keep fiscal responsibility and sustainability in mind at every juncture; how we hire and fire; how we grow. That question is like a moral imperative that keeps us honest. It keeps us on the course we say we want to be on.

We often couple this big question with another litmus test that Jerry puts to us as: How would we feel if our kids worked at our company? Would we be proud of what they would experience? Would we feel good knowing they are safe, well-treated, and being given the opportunity to grow into their fullest, most adult selves?

What surfaces from these inquiries then reverberates into the lists of things to be done, to the hearts showing up with us each day, to how we execute growth. It carries with it our ethos and the experience of the container we set up (the company), and for all the good work we're delivering.

The bigger the decisions we face, the more we sit with these questions. For as anyone who's been coached by one of our coaches knows, there's a power in grappling with such radical self-inquiry. It is, after all, at the very core of who we are at Reboot.

Well-asked questions are not only essential to good coaching but essential to great leadership. They are, in fact, the means to a well-lived life.

We often let these questions speak and rattle around in us a bit, as we work through how to keep ourselves focused on not only what we want, but what's important. They help us hold fast to those anchors so we don't get lost in the friendly noise, suggestions, and shoulds from the outside world.

The questions and issues arising at the heart of our businesses and companies may feel hard, yet rushing through them doesn't make it easier or more graceful. Advice from the external world doesn't always fit either, because the proverbial they aren't living with your specific situation.

So often we heed the questions we face and the decisions we need to make with a frenetic sensibility towards answering them. When we rush through life and the questions we're presented with, how do we create space to be intentional in our decisions, to sit with the important questions at the helm? How can we slow down and sense what's emerging from the questions or chaos or new growth?

It requires a different way of being with things. Sometimes we have to look askew versus straight on at something. Sometimes it pays to tap into other ways of knowing, such as our intuition and gut, versus hiding behind a screen of data or pure intellect. Slowing down allows us to move at a pace different from rapid-fire thoughts and rationalizations. We sense with the largeness of our body, with the fullness of our hearts, to pick up on emergent themes. Our soul comes to take us back—or call us back to what really matters, and what's present for us here.

As you sit with the big questions yourself, I offer you this verse penned by my colleague Jim Marsden that has become the official Reboot poem:

The Question
(an homage to David Whyte's "Self Portrait")

It doesn't matter to me how much you're worth on paper,
or who you know or hang out with.
I want to know what your heart values

and what courage—perhaps dormant—
awaits
inside of you
to dare to pursue that for which your heart truly longs.

It doesn't matter to me how close you are to an IPO,
or if there are whispers of "unicorn" stirring among investors.
I want to know why this business matters to you
and if there's any chance of cultivating
culture, relationships, and business that
brings people—including you—
into their own wholeness and vitality.

And what stops you.

It doesn't matter if your bank account has one zero or many,
I want to know if you're willing to melt
into the fire of why it is that you are you in the first place.
I'm not interested in the litany
of sacrifices and trade-offs
you've made to get here.

What is it that you carry
that cannot and
will not be sacrificed,
no matter what the opportunity
or the promise of salvation?

I'm curious if you know or sense the amazing
power and vitality that comes from
vulnerability
and
awareness
for this being the day to be alive.

And to know that prosperity is to be found in how we live our lives,
not in the spreadsheets and stories
we tell our investors, our colleagues, or ourselves.

I have come to see that those who speak
and step into
the paradox and tension of not knowing
guided by haunting questions of
Where do I go from here?
But how can I? And how can I not?
Who or where am I now?
cross a threshold of not knowing

toward a place where they become aware of things
their body cannot remain unaware of any longer,

where vitality, success and
the joy of simply being human
thrive.

ACKNOWLEDGMENTS

This book is a sum of many parts, and a spawn of many inspirations.

The Reboot newsletter began as a way to introduce the Reboot podcast episodes, which began as conversations with entrepreneurs about the challenges they faced. These were more than practical how-to conversations; they were coaching conversations about the inner work at play for leaders facing these challenges. In addition to pulling themes from these conversations for the newsletters, I'd also pull in themes that surfaced at bootcamps, in our work with clients, books I was reading at the time, poetry, and my own lived experience. For me, the cadence of our newsletter became a creative writing opportunity—a creative challenge to weave in many threads about the human and entrepreneurial experience—and I love me a "create-from-nothing, blank-page" creative challenge. I would trust all the conversations that arose around the theme of a podcast and then gather those threads. There are many people to thank for inspiration—my business partners (Jerry Colonna and Dan Putt), our podcast guests, the poets, Reboot's many clients around the globe, my fellow colleagues and coaches—each providing a golden thread of heart-matter for each piece.

Our newsletters were intended to be offerings—gifts—more than overt marketing material. Folks would tell me that they would stop everything and pause to read each issue when it plopped into their inbox. In a world in which attention is scarce, this was the highest compliment. It also tracked with how I wanted to connect with our audience—that is, as an extension of the work we do as an organization, to be able to stir hearts around the topic of life, work, and meaning. Over time, folks would say, "I wish you'd put these into a book. I don't want to remove them from my inbox." And, ten years into the organization, ta-da! Here we are. Wrapping these up in a book felt like a worthwhile way to commemorate the first decade of Reboot. Thank you to everyone who has followed along or worked with us over the years. Your attention means the world to us, and we appreciate this connection to your hearts.

While this book was essentially written when we set to bind and print it, it took a lot of editing, sorting, arranging, and proofing to get it into a shape where each essay could stand alone in some semblance of a structure. Jerry clued me into Otterpine after reviewing one of their authors' books, and I'm so glad for the ease of that connection. The women who helped usher this book into existence are fantastic humans. Emma Colonna, thank you for compiling all the blog posts into a big Google doc that made it hard to download, but so easy to hand to the editor. Margaret Hendricks, thank you for your clear sight and calm heart and steady support and rhythmic consistency in all of Reboot's content matters, and especially our newsletter missives. Thanks, too, for the pep talks. To the women at Otterpine—Saeah Wood, Amy Reed, Terri Welch, and Laura Tutko—you are masters of your craft and you make the self-publishing process feel like ease and flow (something a company full of women can do so well!).

I've been lucky to learn from and work with masterful practitioners over the years. Heaping scoops of gratitude to Michelle Masters, Carl Buchheit of NLP Marin, and Kelly Wendorf at EQUUS in Santa Fe. Likewise, thanks to James Hollis and Melissa Grace. I'm a firm believer that the best self-help-type books happen because of the good therapists and change-agents behind the author's own development. To Lynda Sexson: all I've learned in your classes at Montana State is always so close, every day, and I am infinitely grateful. To Miriam Meima, Heather Jassy, Cassandra

Field, Liz Stewart, Mom, and Sara for reminding me who I am and loving me for that.

Meeting Jerry in 2013 was most of my wildest dreams arriving at my doorstep in both work and life. Working alongside a good human, doing good work in the world was something I'd been manifesting for quite some time. Reboot has given me the container to exercise my ops chops, develop a leading brand in the coaching space, write-write-write, and learn and grow as a coach and a human. I'm infinitely grateful for our partnership in work and life. Ever since the first bootcamp, we've been creating containers for the soulful magic to happen, giving hearts the space to transform. Here's to the next ten-plus years!

To my Upper Midwestern family of awesome folks: We come from a long line of broken hearts, and we turned out quite well considering. I love all of us and think we're an amazing family. Thanks for always being there and inviting me back in from the barn.

To all the horses I've had the pleasure of caring for since I was a horse-less kid in Eau Claire County's 4-H program, especially my own small herd of beautiful beings, past and present. They remind me that no matter what plan I have, the answer is always relationship over task. A big thanks to Gloria Bloom for getting me started on the right hoof in the horsemanship arena and for taking me to Ray Hunt and Tom Dorrance clinics when I was in middle and high school. A semi-load of many bales of gratitude to the horse persons who are leading the conversation around horse welfare these days, shifting the old dominance theory on its head and grounding the relationship in polyvagal theory instead. As a deep ecologist at heart, it's a welcomed and much needed shift towards an I-Thou sense of the self-other relationship that's reverberating in many arenas on the planet, allowing for better (and much needed) attunement in relationships to all things in and out of the pasture.

BIBLIOGRAPHY

bab.la. "Threshold." Accessed March 19, 2024. https://en.bab.la/dictionary/english/threshold.

Bachelard, Gaston. *The Poetics of Space*. Translated by Maria Jolas. New York: Penguin, 2014.

Bateson, Mary Catherine. "Living as an Improvisational Art." Interview by Krista Tippett. *On Being*, podcast, last modified December 31, 2020. https://onbeing.org/programs/mary-catherine-bateson-living-as-an-improvisational-art/.

Beak, Sera. *Redvelations: A Soul's Journey to Becoming Human*. Louisville: Sounds True, 2018.

Berry, Wendell. *The Unforeseen Wilderness*. Berkeley: Counterpoint, 2006.

Bennis, Warren. *On Being a Leader*. New York: Basic Books, 2009.

Blackie, Sharon. *If Women Rose Rooted*. Tewkesbury: September Publishing, 2019.

Brewer, Judson. *The Craving Mind: From Cigarettes to Smartphones to Love—Why We Get Hooked and How We Can Break Bad Habits*. New Haven: Yale University Press, 2018.

Brewer, Judson. *The Reboot Podcast*. Episode 75, "A Pattern of Habits." Interview by Jerry Colonna. Reboot, January 13, 2018. https://www.reboot.io/episode/75-pattern-habits-judson-brewer/.

Brezsny, Rob. *Pronoia Is the Antidote for Paranoia, Revised and Expanded: How the Whole World Is Conspiring to Shower You with Blessings*. Berkeley: North Atlantic Books, 2009.

Brown, Brené. *Braving the Wilderness: The Quest for True Belonging and the Courage to Stand Alone*. New York: Random House, 2019.

Brown, Brené. *The Gifts of Imperfection*. Center City: Hazelden, 2022.

Brown, Molly Young. *The Unfolding Self: The Practice of Psychosynthesis*. New York: Allworth Press, 2004.

Campbell, Joseph, and Bill Moyers. *The Power of Myth*. New York: Anchor, 1991.

Chödrön, Pema. *Comfortable with Uncertainty: 108 Teachings on Cultivating Fearlessness and Compassion*. Boulder: Shambhala, 2018.

Chödrön, Pema. *When Things Fall Apart: Heart Advice for Difficult Times*. Boulder: Shambhala, 2016.

Colonna, Jerry. *Reboot: Leadership and the Art of Growing Up*. New York: Harper Business, 2019.

Cope, Stephen. *The Great Work of Your Life: A Guide for the Journey to Your True Calling*. New York: Bantam Books, 2015.

Courage & Renewal. "Touchstones." Center for Courage & Renewal. Accessed March 21, 2024. https://couragerenewal.org/wp-content /uploads/2022/10/CCR_Touchstones_V5.pdf.

Cummings, E. E. *A Miscellany*. New York: Liveright, 2018.

Ehrlich, Gretel. *The Solace of Open Spaces*. New York: Penguin, 1986.

Feltman, Charles. *The Thin Book of Trust: An Essential Primer For Building Trust at Work*. Bend: Thin Book Publishing, 2021.

Ferguson, Marilyn. *The Aquarian Conspiracy: Personal and Social Transformation in Our Time*. United States: Jeremy P. Tarcher, 1987.

Gilbert, Elizabeth. *Eat Pray Love*. New York: Riverhead, 2007.

Goleman, Daniel. "Friends for Life: An Emerging Biology of Emotional Healing." *New York Times*, October 10, 2006. https://www.nytimes .com/2006/10/10/health/psychology/10essa.html.

Godin, Seth. *The Reboot Podcast*. Episode 83, "How You Walk Through the World." Interview by Jerry Colonna. Reboot, May 17, 2018. https://www.reboot.io/episode/83-walk-world-seth-godin/.

Grandin, Temple, and Catherine Johnson. *Animals in Translation: Using the Mysteries of Autism to Decode Animal Behavior*. San Diego: Harcourt, 2006.

Graham, Linda. *Bouncing Back: Rewiring Your Brain for Maximum Resilience and Well-Being*. Novato: New World Library, 2013.

Greenleaf Center. "What is Servant Leadership?" Robert K. Greenleaf Center for Servant Leadership. Accessed March 21, 2024. https://www.greenleaf.org/what-is-servant-leadership/.

Hanh, Thich Nhat. *The Art of Power*. San Francisco: HarperOne, 2008.

Harrison, Elle. *Wild Courage: A Journey of Transformation for You and Your Business*. London: Watkins, 1999.

Hellinger, Bert, Gunthard Weber, and Hunter Beaumont. *Love's Hidden Symmetry: What Makes Love Work in Relationships*. Phoenix: Zeig Tucker & Theisen Inc., 1998.

Hollis, James. *Hauntings: Dispelling Ghosts Who Run Our Lives*. Asheville: Chiron Publications, 2015.

Hollis, James. *The Eden Project: In Search of the Magical Other*. Ontario: Inner City Books, 1998.

Hollis, James. *The Middle Passage: From Misery to Meaning in Midlife*. Ontario: Inner City Books, 1993.

Hollis, James. *Through the Dark Wood: Finding Meaning in the Second Half of Life*. Louisville: Sounds True, 2009.

Hollis, James. *What Matters Most: Living a More Considered Life*. New York: Avery, 2009.

Hollis, James. *Why Good People Do Bad Things: Understanding Our Darker Selves*. New York: Penguin, 2008.

Houston, Jean. *A Mythic Life: Learning to Live Our Greater Story*. San Francisco: HarperOne, 1996.

Jacobs, Jason. *The Reboot Podcast*. Episode 68, "Your Second Act." Interview by Jerry Colonna. *Reboot*, September 21, 2017. https://www.reboot.io/episode/68-second-act-jason-jacobs/.

Johnson, Spencer, and Steven Pileggi. *The Value of Believing in Yourself: The Story of Louis Pasteur*. La Jolla: Value Communications, 1976.

Jung, Carl. *Psychology and Alchemy*. Translated by Gerhard Adler and R. F. C. Hull. Princeton: Princeton University Press, 1980.

Kabat-Zinn, Jon. *Wherever You Go, There You Are*. New York: Hachette Books, 2005.

Kean, Amy. *The Little Girl Who Gave Zero F*cks*. London: Unbound, 2020.

Kohanov, Linda. *Power of the Herd: A Nonpredatory Approach to Social Intelligence, Leadership, and Innovation*. Novato: New World Library, 2015.

Kübler-Ross, Elisabeth. *On Death and Dying: What the Dying Have to Teach Doctors, Nurses, Clergy and Their Own Families*. New York: Scribner, 2014.

Lamott, Anne. *Plan B: Further Thoughts on Faith*. New York: Riverhead, 2006.

Lanier, Heather Kirn. "Superbabies Don't Cry." *Vela*, April 7, 2017. http://velamag.com/superbabies-dont-cry/.

Lawrence, D. H. *Phoenix: The Posthumous Papers of D. H. Lawrence*. New York: The Viking Press, 1936.

Lesser, Elizabeth. *Broken Open: How Difficult Times Can Help Us Grow*. New York: Villard, 2005.

Lencioni, Patrick. *The Five Dysfunctions of a Team: A Leadership Fable*. Hoboken: Jossey-Bass, 2002.

MacIver, Roderick. *Art as a Way of Life*. Berkeley: North Atlantic Books, 2009.

Mackesy, Charlie. *The Boy, the Mole, the Fox and the Horse*. San Francisco: HarperOne, 2019.

Meade, Michael. *Why the World Doesn't End: Tales of Renewal in Times of Loss*. Housatonic: Green Fire Press, 2012.

Merton, Thomas. *The Wisdom of the Desert*. New York: New Directions, 1970.

Moore, Thomas. *Care of the Soul: A Guide for Cultivating Depth and Sacredness in Everyday Life*. New York: Harper Perennial, 2016.

Nouwen, Henri J. M. *Bread for the Journey: A Daybook of Wisdom and Faith*. San Francisco: HarperOne, 2006.

Obama, Michelle. *Becoming*. New York: Crown, 2021.

O'Donohue, John. *Conamara Blues: Poems*. New York: Harper Perennial, 2004.

O'Donohue, John. *Eternal Echoes: Celtic Reflections on Our Yearning to Belong*. New York: Harper Perennial, 2000.

O'Donohue, John. *To Bless the Space Between Us: A Book of Blessings*. New York: Doubleday, 2008.

O'Donohue, John. "John O'Donohue at Greenbelt." Greenbelt Festival, August 2007. Video by John R. Finch. YouTube, uploaded June 24, 2014. https://www.youtube.com/watch?v=iDSw5Vza6Yk.

Orlowski, Jeff. *The Reboot Podcast*. Episode 73, "Chasing Purpose." Interview by Jerry Colonna. Reboot, December 14, 2017. https://www.reboot.io/episode/73-chasing-purpose-jeff-orlowski/.

Palmer, Parker J. *The Courage to Teach: Exploring the Inner Landscape of a Teacher's Life*. Hoboken: Jossey-Bass, 2017.

Palmer, Parker J. *Let Your Life Speak*. Hoboken: Jossey-Bass, 1999.

Palmer, Parker J. *The Reboot Podcast*. Episode 42, "Building Relational Trust." Interview by Jerry Colonna. *Reboot*, June 12, 2016. https://www.reboot.io/episode/42-building-relational-trust-parker-palmer/.

Pieri, Jules. *How We Make Stuff Now: Turn Ideas into Products That Build Successful Businesses*. New York: McGraw Hill, 2019.

Plotkin, Bill. *Soulcraft: Crossing into the Mysteries of Nature and Psyche*. Novato: New World Library, 2003.

Plotkin, Bill. *Wild Mind: A Field Guide to the Human Psyche*. Novato: New World Library, 2013.

Pressfield, Steven. *The War of Art: Break Through the Blocks and Win Your Inner Creative Battles*. New York: Black Irish Entertainment LLC, 2012.

Remen, Rachel Naomi. *Kitchen Table Wisdom: Stories That Heal*. New York: Riverhead, 2006.

Richo, David. *How to Be an Adult in Love: Letting Love in Safely and Showing It Recklessly*. Boulder: Shambhala, 2014.

Richo, David. *How to Be an Adult in Relationships: The Five Keys to Mindful Loving*. Boulder: Shambhala, 2021.

Richo, David. *Shadow Dance: Liberating the Power and Creativity of Your Dark Side*. Boulder: Shambhala, 2024.

Richo, David. *You Are Not What You Think: The Egoless Path to Self-Esteem and Generous Love*. Boulder: Shambhala, 2015.

Robbins, Tom. *Another Roadside Attraction*. New York: Bantam Books, 1991.

Rogers, Fred. *You Are Special: Neighborly Words of Wisdom from Mister Rogers*. United States: Penguin Publishing Group, 1995.

Rohr, Richard. *Falling Upward: A Spirituality for the Two Halves of Life*. Hoboken: Jossey-Bass, 2023.

Roth, Gabrielle, John Loudon, and Angeles Arrien. *Maps to Ecstasy: The Healing Power of Movement*. Novato: New World Library, 1998.

Rumi, Jalal al-Din. *The Essential Rumi*. Translated by Coleman Barks and John Moyne. San Francisco: HarperOne, 2004.

Ryan, David. *The Reboot Podcast*. Episode 104, "The Next Chapter." Interview by Jerry Colonna. *Reboot*, May 10, 2019. https://www.reboot.io/episode/104-the-next-chapter-with-david-ryan/.

Ryokan. *One Robe, One Bowl: The Zen Poetry of Ryokan*. Translated by John Stevens. New York: Weatherhill, 1977.

Salzberg, Sharon. "Getting Over Guilt." *On Being*, November 16, 2015. https://onbeing.org/blog/getting-over-guilt/.

Salzberg, Sharon. "How to Talk with Your Relatives over the Holidays." *On Being*, November 17, 2017. https://onbeing.org/blog/sharon-salzberg-how-to-talk-with-your-relatives-over-the-holidays/.

Salzberg, Sharon. *Real Love: The Art of Mindful Connection*. New York: Flatiron Books, 2018.

Salzberg, Sharon. *Lovingkindness: The Revolutionary Art of Happiness*. Boulder: Shambhala, 2018.

Schnarch, David. *Passionate Marriage: Keeping Love and Intimacy Alive in Committed Relationships*. New York: W. W. Norton & Company, 2009.

Selye, Hans. *The Stress of Life*. New York: McGraw Hill, 1978.

Spolsky, Joel. "The Management Team - Guest Post From Joel Spolsky." *AVC*, February 13, 2012. https://mba-mondays-illustrated.com/2015/04/the-management-team-guest-post-from-joel-spolsky/

Watterson, Meggan. *Mary Magdalene Revealed: The First Apostle, Her Feminist Gospel & the Christianity We Haven't Tried Yet.* Carlsbad: Hay House Inc., 2019.

Watts, Alan. *The Culture of Counter-Culture: The Edited Transcripts.* Boston: C. E. Tuttle Company, 1998.

Watts, Alan. *This Is It: And Other Essays on Zen and Spiritual Experience.* New York: Vintage, 1973.

Welwood, John. *Challenge of the Heart: Love, Sex, and Intimacy in Changing Times.* Boulder: Shambhala, 1985.

Whyte, David. *Fire in the Earth.* Langley: Many Rivers Press, 1992.

Whyte, David. *The Heart Aroused: Poetry and the Preservation of the Soul in Corporate America.* New York: Crown Currency, 1996.

williams, angel Kyodo. "The World Is Our Field of Practice." Interview by Krista Tippett. *On Being*, podcast, last modified September 10, 2020. https://onbeing.org/programs/angel-kyodo-williams-the-world-is-our-field-of-practice/.

Williams, Terry Tempest. *When Women Were Birds: Fifty-Four Variations on Voice.* London: Picador, 2013.

Woodman, Marion. "Worshipping Illusions: An Interview with Marion Woodman." Interview by Parabola Editors. *Parabola*, April 13, 2019. https://parabola.org/2019/04/13/worshipping-illusions-an-interview-with-marion-woodman/.

ABOUT THE AUTHOR

Soul, savvy, magic, heart. These are the ways Allison Schultz moves in the world.

In 2014, after years of work in a variety of startups and a lifetime of soul-based explorations, Ali co-founded Reboot.io. As co-founder and coach, Ali weaves her business acumen with the innate wisdom of the body, the philosophies of the world's wisdom traditions, and the "way of the horse" to help clients find their voice in service of finding themselves.

A visionary in the leadership development space, Ali cut her teeth in the early 2000s in the Boulder startup scene where she worked as an operator developing brands and managing projects, teams, and human resources. In 2013, she and Jerry Colonna partnered to create the life-changing CEO and Founder Bootcamp, held throughout the US and abroad, that laid the foundation for the work that would become Reboot.

Ali is driven by the conviction that creating humane workplaces of safety and connection is an inside job that begins within each of us. Core to her work is the belief that whatever situation you're in, the most important conversation you can have is the one with your own heart, and the most important relationship you have is the one you have with yourself.

Ali has a master's degree in religious studies from the University of Colorado at Boulder, studied Transformational Neuro-linguistic Programming at NLP Marin, and is a certified EQUUS Experience Facilitator.

ADDITIONAL RESOURCES

For more resources, visit reboot.io or scan the QR code below.

You'll find many free self-guided courses, more practical content, and a free 365-day journal course that pairs well with this book.

You can follow the author on Instagram @thedeeppeaceproject and on Twitter @manifestcookies.

You can follow Reboot @reboothq.

For fan mail, coaching, and bulk order requests, email ali@reboot.io.

www.ingramcontent.com/pod-product-compliance
Lightning Source LLC
Chambersburg PA
CBHW030402130626
46549CB00004B/1599